CHARTERED COMPANIES

CHARTERED COMPANIES

and their Role in the Development
of Overseas Trade

★

RUDOLPH ROBERT

LONDON
G. BELL AND SONS, LTD
1969

Published by
G. BELL AND SONS, LTD
York House, Portugal St.,
London, W.C.2

SBN 7135 1524 4
PRINTED IN GREAT BRITAIN BY
MORRISON AND GIBB LIMITED, LONDON AND EDINBURGH

Contents

Illustrations

Acknowledgments

THREE of the companies whose histories are traced in the
following pages are still very much alive. My first thanks,
therefore, must go to them, i.e. the British South Africa
Company (now a part of the Charter Consolidated Group) for
information supplied, and to the Hudson's Bay Company and
the Falkland Islands Company for granting access to material,
some of it not elsewhere available, for the loan of photographs,
and for reading through, and suggesting amendments to, my
draft chapters.

I am also appreciative of the assistance given me in the
course of my researches by the staff of the British Museum
Reading Room, who have in their keeping the minute books,
account books, and papers of the South Sea Company, and
many other relevant records. The specialist library of the
Chartered Institute of Secretaries, with its unrivalled collection
of company histories of all kinds, has also proved invaluable.
I thank the librarian of the Institute for help most readily
given.

Finally, I have to acknowledge my heavy debt to the innumerable authorities whom I had of necessity to consult in
the course of preparing this book. The most useful, from the
student's point of view, are indicated in the Select Bibliography
at the end. Some of the older writers are long since out of
print, others have been outmoded, at least on points of detail,
as the result of modern research. Some have stressed the
elements of romance—by no means lacking—in their narratives.
Others have laid emphasis on dry-as-dust financial and
statistical detail. Among the wheat, it must be admitted, is a
good deal of chaff. Nevertheless, in its totality the literature is
very impressive, wide-ranging, and full of unsuspected treasures.
For that everyone who approaches the subject afresh, as I have
ventured to do, must be grateful.

R. R.

*Trading in Companies is most Agreeable
to the English Nature*

SIR FRANCIS BACON

* 1 *

The Beginnings and Development of the Joint Stock Company

THERE have been companies, in the sense of associations of traders co-operating for some particular purpose, ever since the dawn of civilization. This must necessarily have been so, for two or three men combining their resources— whether to equip a Phoenician galley or a Samarkandian camel-train— make a stronger unit than one man alone. It must have been early discovered that the league, or fellowship, was essential if attacks from bandits and pirates were to be resisted, and if trade was to be conducted on a worth-while and orderly basis.

One of the precursors of the joint stock company in England was the merchant-guild, a medieval institution that had the right to regulate trade in the towns and villages. The merchants forming it bought all that was consumed, and sold all that was produced, by the communities they served. Often the members of such a merchant-guild were the burgesses of a town that had won its freedom from the manorial overlord as the result of a royal charter.

The merchant-guilds were at their most influential in the thirteenth century, by which time their aim was little more than to secure for their members a monopoly of all commercial dealings. The merchant who did not belong to the guild, in the few cases where he was allowed to trade at all, was hedged about with restrictions and required to pay heavy tolls.

Trade by retail in certain goods—wool, cloth, leather, meat and fish—was altogether prohibited to outsiders, and the guildsmen not only regulated sales but claimed an option on all purchasable goods, in small or large quantities, that became available. In fact, a basic object of the merchant-guild was to secure monopolistic privileges, and to maintain such privileges against all challengers, whether from within the city walls or from outside. This tradition carried over into later centuries, and it is a feature of nearly all the early company formations that they sought to exploit some exclusive right, as, for example, a manufacturing process, or the trade with a foreign country.

It would not be wholly accurate, however, to say that the merchant-guilds were mere combinations of businessmen bent on furthering their own ends at the general expense. They had their code of ethics and were forbidden to speculate or indulge in sharp practices.

II

A raw material of considerable importance in medieval times was wool, which not only yielded substantial revenues to the Crown but played its part in shaping foreign policy. Parliament in 1275 granted King Edward I the right to levy an export duty on wool, and two years later a group of traders, known as the Merchants of the Staple, commenced its activities. The wool exports were placed under its control, and when the Staple was moved to Calais, at the time when Normandy was still with the English Crown, the merchants assumed responsibility for the customs, for the Government of the town, and for paying the garrison. They developed into a powerful monopoly, and have interest as an early form of company organization.

Somewhat similar in status was the famous body known as the Merchant Adventurers, which sprang into prominence when wool's importance had declined and finished cloth had taken its place as the main item of English manufacture and export. There was, however, a difference between them and the Staplers, for the Merchant Adventurers were a 'regulated' company, incorporated by royal charter. Their association, dating from 1505, was free-and-easy, each individual adventurer being allowed to trade on his own account, as in the merchant guild. The principle of contributing capital into a common pool, and of sharing profits or losses, had yet to win general acceptance. Nevertheless, it was but a step from an association such as that of the Merchant Adventurers to the true joint stock company—particularly as in practice many of the Adventurers had entered into partnership with others, thus forming a number of 'embryonic' joint stocks.

III

However, it was not until the times of Henry VIII and Queen Elizabeth I that joint stock companies, clearly recognizable as such, emerged and began to function. The Russia Company, reputedly the first, was formed in 1553 by a group of capitalists with the object of discovering the 'unknown lands in the north'. What they discovered was Russia, and the trade that followed was by no means unprofitable.

Half a century later, on 31st December 1600, the East India Company embarked upon its astonishing career. This, too, differed radically from the combinations of merchants that had flourished a century earlier. From the first it broke completely with the tradition of the 'regulated' company, and organized its finances on a collective basis. The members did not trade as individuals, but each merchant or 'adventurer' subscribed to the capital fund just so much as he thought fit, and received a profit, or suffered a loss, in direct proportion to that capital subscription.

There was probably a certain caution and hesitancy in accepting the new form of organization for, at first, the joint stocks were *ad hoc* arrangements—entered into for a single voyage. Only as the principle of a common capital gradually vindicated itself in practice were the subscriptions extended to cover several voyages. Finally, in 1657, when the last doubts had been removed, investments in the East India Company were made on a permanent basis—with the one proviso that shareholders could, if they so desired, transfer their holdings to third parties.

The East India Company, like the Russia Company, applied for a royal charter and monopoly privileges, both considered indispensable in those days, and was granted the whole of the trade to and from the East Indies, other merchants being forbidden to engage in the said trade except under the Company's licence. How this all worked out in practice makes one of the most enthralling stories in English economic history.

The potentialities of the chartered companies having been recognized, it was not long before others were formed: in fact, a veritable spate of company flotations took place in the late sixteenth and early seventeenth centuries—a fair number of them for trading overseas. One of the most remarkable was formed in 1670, the Hudson's Bay Company, which opened up the territory now known as Canada to English trade.

IV

By the end of the seventeenth century it was obvious, despite strong opposition, that the joint stocks were a useful form of economic organisation and had come to stay. In 1694, during the reign of William and Mary, they scored a triumph such as they have hardly repeated since. A group of City merchants, in return for a loan to the Government, was granted the right to found a central bank such as the Dutch already had. The Bank of England, as it turned out, was a success, and remained a joint stock company, incorporated by royal charter, until 1946, when it was nationalized.

Though the joint stock principle was extended to apply not only to overseas ventures but to manufacture and internal trade, the companies were not, of course, invariably successful. They had their ups and downs, and large profits in some years were offset by equally large losses in others. Dealings in shares—'stock-jobbing' as it was called—also opened the way to abuses that had not existed in earlier days.

The crash of the South Sea Company, in 1720, was failure on a catastrophic scale. Just prior to it, a speculative fever had forced the Company's shares up to fantastically high levels, a belief having gained widespread acceptance that wealth, by a mystique known only to the financiers, could be spun out of thin air. When this general illusion about the nature of 'credit' had been dispelled, and the Bubble pricked, there was bitterness and panic throughout the land.

The Government, itself partly to blame, was obliged to intervene, to bring the recreant directors of the South Sea Company to book, and to prohibit the formation of more mushroom concerns of the kind that had sprung up in the boom and intensified the effects of the crash. An Act was passed through Parliament, the so-called 'Bubble Act', which made it illegal to form joint stock companies in future except by means of a royal charter.

The South Sea Company had, of course, been legitimately incorporated in that way, but most of the other Bubble companies had not. As a result of the new legislation, joint stock company development was inevitably retarded. Royal charters were not only difficult to obtain, but expensive, and so for more than a hundred years the most usual form of commercial association was the partnership.

One other point needs to be mentioned: even the earliest chartered companies appear to have enjoyed the privilege of limited liability i.e. each individual member's liability ceased when he had fully paid up his share.

V

The eighteenth century was one of those periods when the historic process, usually slow-moving as the Thames at Windsor, hurls itself over a series of Niagara Falls and attains truly dynamic power and speed. The Agrarian and Industrial Revolutions took place. A brief half-century, from 1750 to 1800, saw the entire human prospect changed. Many problems were, of course, posed by the sudden advance, one of the most pressing being that of improving poor communications and bringing the new mills and factories closer to the markets in which their products could be sold. And it was in connection with communications that the joint stock companies were to experience their next great upsurge. Hundreds of companies were formed for the purpose of constructing a network of canals. Hardly had this frenzy expended itself than another, that was to last longer and have more permanent effect, seized the investing public. Canal construction was replaced by a mania for railway building.

The companies that undertook these great projects were of a different kind from those so far considered. Their main concern was not with trade but with works of a public nature. Such companies derived their authority from the Government; they were incorporated by special Acts of Parliament, a separate Act being necessary for each specific undertaking. The statutory company does not, of course, make any radical departure from the chartered company: in principle and practice it is the same—a form of joint stock enterprise.

VI

As we have seen, company development was virtually arrested after passing of the Bubble Act in 1719, for it became an indictable offence for a company to invite public subscriptions, to make its stock transferable, or to act as a body corporate except on the basis of a royal charter. The Act, passed with the best of intentions for the protection of the public, remained in force until after the end of the Napoleonic Wars, when a great deal of capital was free for investment, and an entirely new situation had arisen. Eventually, in 1825, Parliament repealed the Bubble Act, and the 'unincorporated' companies that had been formed were treated as partnerships.

As such they could neither sue nor be sued unless all their members were joined in the legal proceedings. Companies with large memberships were, as a result, virtually barred from going to the courts, a circumstance that gave rise to many difficulties. An Act was, therefore, passed in 1834, empowering the Crown to give unincorporated companies the right of maintaining actions in the names of their officers. Both this Act and the Act of 1825 were repealed in 1837, their place being taken by the Joint Stock Companies Act of 1844, the first to deal with the subject on a comprehensive scale. This Act of 1844 sought to end abuses of various kinds, and provided for compulsory registration of joint stock companies, which were defined as all partnerships of more than twenty-five persons and partnerships with transferable shares.

Though the incorporation of joint stock companies then became a right instead of a privilege, for all practical purposes they still remained partnerships with unlimited liability. This left the company promoters and entrepreneurs with a major problem still unsolved.

VII

Parliament at that time rejected the idea of trading by manufacturing companies whose liability was limited; and, in fact, ten years elapsed before the climate of opinion changed. Not until 1854 did the House of Commons pass the resolution that fathered the Limited Liability Act of 1855, which finally established the important principle that joint stock companies could limit their liability to the amounts unpaid on their shares.

Another important legislative landmark was the Companies Act of 1862—intended to be a comprehensive code of law applicable to trading companies for the whole of the United Kingdom. Experience had shown the disadvantages of permitting trading activities to be carried on by bodies whose membership changed from day to day. Hence one of the Act's first and most stringent provisions: that no company, association or partnership consisting of more than twenty persons (or ten in the case of banking) should be formed for the purpose of carrying on any business for the acquisition of gain unless it was registered.

Companies formed in pursuance of an Act of Parliament or of letters patent, or companies engaged in working mines within, and subject to the jurisdiction of, the Stannaries* were exempt from the provisions. Fundamentally, the main concern of the Act was that all commercial undertakings—as distinct from learned, charitable, or other non-profit-making bodies— should be registered. Having made its intentions clear, the Act went on to specify the precise way in which companies were to be incorporated. Briefly, it was laid down that any seven or more persons associated for any legal purpose could, by

* The *Stannaries* are the districts comprising the tin mines of Cornwall and Devon (Latin *stannum* = tin) which, by virtue of ancient charters, are exempt from all jurisdiction other than that of Stannary courts. The Stannary Courts Abolition Act of 1896 transferred their jurisdiction to the county courts. Companies working tin mines in Cornwall are, in effect, partnerships.

subscribing their names to a memorandum of association, form a company with or without limited liability. The document to be subscribed—the form of which was given in a schedule to the Act—corresponded to the charter or deed of settlement in the case of other corporations.

Considered in its entirety, the Companies Act of 1862 is important in that it laid the foundations of company law as we know it today. There have been subsequent reshapings, amendments and alterations. Two major consolidating Acts were passed in 1928 and 1948, and further modifications following upon the report of the Jenkins Committee in 1962, are pending. Yet many of the basic principles remain, and are likely to remain, unchanged.

VIII

The Victorian company legislation certainly had a liberating effect. Once that the right to incorporate, without recourse to a royal charter or Act of Parliament, and the principle of limited liability were recognized, the numbers of joint stock companies rapidly increased. Some of those that sprang up had short lives and quickly passed into oblivion. Others, both small and large, have survived to the present day. The phenomenal rate of the development is apparent from the Board of Trade statistics, which reveal that at 31st December 1964 there were 512,590 public and private companies at work in this country.

Their diversity of purpose, structure, and size is truly extraordinary. At one end of the scale is the small private company controlled, in effect, by a single person and making anything from brass buttons to bedsteads. At the other end of the scale is the giant combine, sometimes monopolistic in character, integrated vertically or horizontally, sustained in its activities, which may range from soap-making to battleship construction, by two great armies—of workers and shareholders. We have witnessed, since the beginning of the present century, the growth of joint stock companies that control whole families of subsidiaries and sub-subsidiaries. This modern tendency to merge and amalgamate into enormous industrial power-blocks may be deplored, for it can lead to abuse, but is nevertheless inevitable in an age of mass production. So fierce is the struggle to lower costs and capture markets that only the leviathans can survive.

Since the end of the Second World War the State has, of course, taken over a number of important industries—transport, coal, gas, and electricity—formerly organized on a joint stock basis. That, too, is a significant development, for it prompts the question: Has the joint stock company, the 'association of individuals possessing a common stock' reached, or even perhaps passed, the zenith of its usefulness? Is it doomed, like the dinosaurs, to extinction? Or can it yet rise to higher things?

These are among the major economic issues of our day, and even the most tentative answer would involve a great deal of speculation, of controversial politics, and sociological fortune-telling. On the basis of past history this, however, may be safely said: the joint stock companies have shown themselves to be highly adaptable to environmental change, however radical. They have displayed commendable initiative in pioneering overseas ventures, in developing British manufactures, communications, and inventions. They are versatile, resourceful, and resilient; and some of the best of them have demonstrated a remarkable capacity for survival. The Hudson's Bay Company, which holds the record for longevity, is now nearly three hundred years old.

* 2 *

The Fellowship of
the Merchant Adventurers

FOR the beginnings of English mercantile prosperity we have to look back as far as the thirteenth century, when the Netherlands and other European countries first looked to us for their raw wool supplies. In time, so considerable did the export of wool become that monarchs found it a convenient means of adding considerable sums to their revenue. Staples were set up, i.e. clearing houses through which the wool had to pass for convenience in levying the duties, and a body known as the 'Merchant Staplers' was appointed to regulate wool distribution abroad.

Already at that time we hear of another group—the Merchant Adventurers, who later sprang into prominence, chiefly in connection with the export of partly finished cloth. They may, possibly, have been an offshoot of the Staplers, for the Merchant Adventurers were trading, from their base at Antwerp, as far back as 1296, in which year the Duke of Brabant granted them a charter.

A great deal of information regarding the early history of the Merchant Adventurers may be gleaned from *The Treatise of Commerce* published in 1601 by John Wheeler, who was both their secretary and historian. The Company thought highly of him, and one of the Governors described him to Robert Cecil as a man 'both wise and honest . . . long acquainted with the manners of the Netherlanders, whose language he hath as perfect as English . . . with a good taste of Latin, French, Italian and Greek' and, above all, a shrewd knowledge of business affairs. According to John Wheeler, Edward III encouraged the Merchant Adventurers by confirming certain privileges they had enjoyed, and in 1360, under their Governor John Wadewayn, they were operating in Flanders in a corporate capacity. The monarch who placed the Merchant Adventurers of England on the road to power and riches was, however, Henry VII who in 1505 granted them a charter consolidating and extending their authority in connection with foreign trade.

Much energy was wasted, early in the Fellowship's existence, in struggles against the Merchant Staplers, who were the chief wool exporters. The Merchant Adventurers, specializing in the export of cloth, tried to force them into a merger, to pay the admission fees and to refrain, as an association, from dealings in cloth. These were demands that the Staplers flatly rejected, as they considered that Staple merchandise was not restricted to wool, but included cloth, in which they had established a regular export trade. The struggle ended in the defeat of the Staplers in the first quarter of the sixteenth century.

A far more dangerous rival, however, had yet to be vanquished. The great confederation of merchants known as the Hanseatic League, with headquarters at Hamburg and Lübeck, was making its own bid for a lion's share of the European trade. Since 1266 the Hanse merchants had been established in London in the Steelyard—which stood on the site now occupied by Cannon Street station. In accounts of the medieval City it is described as a building with 'a fine hall and courtyard'. Its name, 'the Steelyard', was probably derived from the steel beam or 'yard' used for weighing the various goods imported into London—hemp, wax, corn, linen, and so on. The League had similar depots, or *Kontore* (counting houses), at Cologne, Bruges, Bergen, Novgorod, Breslau, Cracow and, when at the height of its power, sixty other cities. Its prosperity, however, was largely based on its monopoly of the Baltic trade.

This conflict between the Merchant Adventurers and the Hanseatic League was very long-drawn-out and bitter. Each fought for a foothold in the other's market; neither appears to have understood the principle of compromise or was prepared to give as well as take. At last, during the reign of Elizabeth I, in 1598, a decisive turning point was reached. The merchants of the Hanseatic League were deprived of the privileges they had enjoyed in England at least since the time of Edward III (to whom they had lent money), their London Steelyard was closed down, and they were placed on the same footing as all other foreign traders.

II

This drastic action had been long and persistently agitated for by the English merchants who considered the preferential treatment accorded to the Hansards as outdated and unfair, all the more so as their own privileged position in the Netherlands had been under attack. The Dutch merchants wanted the special status conferred on the Merchant Adventurers annulled, and proposed that the two nations should trade as equals, without any favours in regard to customs or facilities on either side. It was in 1563, when Philip II of Spain prohibited the importation of cloth and wool into the Netherlands, on the pretext of a pestilence in England, that the controversy first flared into open conflict. The age-old commerce, recognized as highly beneficial to both countries, ground to a standstill, and the Merchant Adventurers, declaring defiantly that 'Antwerp was not indispensable', looked for another base-town from which to conduct their trade.

Two German towns, Hamburg and Emden, hastened to offer hospitality to the English Company, the presence of which was guaranteed to bring them not only honour and prestige but profit. Emden, a port at the mouth of the River Ems, was chosen and arrangements were made for the settlement of the Fellowship in East Friesland, where it was agreed that its members should be allowed to trade free of all customs and excise. Antwerp, when it came to the point, was loth to see the Merchant Adventurers go; and by spreading rumours of various kinds even persuaded some of the more faint-hearted among them to stay. However, the majority transferred to Emden, and by May, 1564, a sizeable English merchant-fleet sailed into the harbour with cargoes of cloth and 'kersies' (coarse narrow cloths woven from long wool and usually ribbed).

At first everything went well; the Merchant Adventurers were cordially received at Emden, but the town unfortunately failed to attract buyers in sufficient numbers, and before the summer was over the Adventurers had departed. Antwerp then tried to negotiate their return, and in fact persuaded them to do so for a time, in order that a dialogue could be held and mutual grievances ventilated. The outbreak of a religious war in the Netherlands and other unsettling factors finally convinced them that they must seek another residence. Hamburg had shown many signs of friendship, and had actually suggested to Queen Elizabeth that, though a Hanse stronghold, it should become the main Continental centre for the distribution of English cloth.

Hamburg, therefore, was decided upon, and in 1567, after a ten-year agreement between the city and the Fellowship had been signed, the Merchant Adventurers left the Netherlands and moved into a German headquarters. It was a major triumph, for in Hamburg the Company—despite all the Hanseatic League's objections—was conceded many special rights and privileges. Houses were built for members at the city's expense, they were assured freedom of religious worship, and promised compensation should they sustain injury at the hands of any German subject. No effort, indeed, was spared to ensure their personal comfort or to promote the prosperity of their trade.

As it happened, the Merchant Adventurers' move to Hamburg was made just in the nick of time, for in 1568 Elizabeth forced a political breach with the Netherlands and their position in Antwerp would then have been untenable— for the Duke of Alba, the tyrannical Spanish Governor, promptly arrested the English merchants who had remained, confiscated their property, and threw them into prison.

III

Whence, it may be asked at this point, did this Company of English Merchant Adventurers derive its authority? How was it constituted, capitalized and governed? Was it in fact a company at all in the accepted sense?

As to their authority and constitution: the Merchant Adventurers based themselves and their trading activities on charters granted by various monarchs over a lengthy period. Henry VII in 1505 had granted them a charter, but the move to Hamburg and the claim to monopoly of the trade with Germany clearly called for its reconsideration and revision. In fact Elizabeth, in 1564, granted the Merchant Adventurers an entirely new charter which incorporated them, in the picturesque terminology of the age, as 'one perpetual fellowship and body politic', and confirmed the new territorial limits within which they were permitted to operate. This document makes it clear that the Merchant Adventurers were, indeed, a company—the first of its kind—a corporation in which, because of its commitment to overseas trade, the State had a vital interest. It was not, however, a joint stock company, with a pooled capital and transferable shares.

Actually, the Merchant Adventurers, as already indicated, belonged to the group of old-style regulated companies, which required their members to trade individually, each providing his own capital, bearing the brunt of his own losses and retaining his own profits. The modern parallel is, of course, the trade association. However, it may be noticed here that within the main body of merchants were smaller groupings, of perhaps five or six, who for reasons of convenience did combine their resources, and these subsidiary groupings, or partnerships, may well be regarded as 'embryo joint stocks'.

With regard to the management of the Fellowship: this, too, was based on clauses in the Elizabethan charter. The seat of government was nominally in the principal mart-town abroad, but in practice power lay effectively in the hands of the London general court, which consisted of a Governor (elected annually by the Continental brethren), a Deputy Governor and twenty-four assistants. Under the terms of the charter, the general court was invested with considerable authority. It could fine and imprison law-breakers; it could at its discretion levy taxes, contributions and tolls on members and their goods.

On the other hand, it was under an obligation to render

assistance to any brother who might be in need of protection and to help him to maintain his rights and privileges under the charter.

IV

Admission to the Fellowship of the Merchant Adventurers could be achieved by one of four methods: by right of birth (i.e. being the son of a Merchant Adventurer), by way of apprenticeship, by purchase, and by free gift. The most important of these was admission by apprenticeship, which involved serving eight years under a 'free brother', and complying with a number of strictly enforced conditions. The apprentice had to be at least sixteen years of age; he was required to serve his master well and truly, to refrain from marriage during the term of his apprenticeship, to act honestly and be of good behaviour. Masters, for their part, were severely restricted as to the number of apprentices they could take into their service. For the first seven years they were allowed only one apprentice—after twenty years in the Fellowship they could take up to three.

When the apprentice, at the age of twenty-four or over, had completed his training he was entitled to claim membership, but again only after certain conditions had been fulfilled. He had to be a loyal subject of the sovereign, he must not have committed crime or perjury, he must have paid to the Company all debts, duties, fines and assessments for which his father or master had been liable and left unpaid. He must have proved himself a person of upright character.

The writ of the Company came into force most rigidly when members were stationed abroad. Under the formidable set of rules which then applied, they were forbidden to lodge in taverns or inns of dubious repute, to indulge in acts of immorality, to gamble or drink to excess. They were forbidden to call another brother 'by approbrious names', to act violently towards other members of the Fellowship, to show disrespect to the Governor, or do anything liable to bring the Company into disrepute or imperil its privileged status. Marriage to foreign women and the acquisition of estates when abroad were other actions that the Fellowship tried to prohibit—not always, in regard to the former, too successfully. Among the more positive rules which had to be observed was conformity to established religion, and anyone who absented himself from church services too often could be disciplined.

Among the *Laws, Customs and Ordinances of the Fellowship of Merchant Adventurers*, as recorded by secretary Wheeler, was one that specifically excluded from membership any person engaged in retail trade. This rule, acceptable to the London merchants, met with considerable opposition in the provinces, particularly in the north—for example, at Newcastle and York—where most of the merchants kept retail shops. This particular ban was partly based on the concept, deeply embedded in the medieval mind, of 'one man one trade', and partly on the belief that English commodities must necessarily be cheapened, and foreign products made dearer, if too many 'unskilled in merchandise' on a large scale were allowed to adventure overseas. There was also, of course, the argument that it was unfair that a man who had served an eight-year apprenticeship to a trade—'wherein was more skill than every man judges'—should have his living prejudiced by the untrained and ignorant.

What the Merchant Adventurers tried to do, in fact, was to raise commerce to the status of a skilled profession and make foreign trade a 'closed shop'. This they were only partially successful in doing—for the prohibition against members who were retailers proved to be unenforceable outside London, and had to be abandoned. They also had to deal, as we shall see later, with the unlicensed traders or 'interlopers'.

V

As a fraternity with a common interest, the Merchant Adventurers had formulated a complex system of rules and regulations for conducting the commerce abroad. No member, for example, was allowed to trade outside of the recognized 'mart towns'—and any breach of that rule could be punished with heavy fines or might even, in extreme cases, lead to expulsion. Another interesting proviso was that all merchandise had to be exported in ships specially chartered by the Company, which sailed in convoy at set times of the year. Spring, summer, autumn and winter marts were held on the Continent but major shipments of cloth were seldom made more than twice annually. Provisions and certain other commodities—including munitions, bow staves and books—could be shipped whenever necessity arose. Usually, the merchants attended the marts in person, and their dealings were, of course, confined to wholesale transactions; for they were as averse to trading retail themselves as to admitting retailers—who were despised as 'vulgar pedlars'—into their ranks.

One other ordinance of the Merchant Adventurers may be mentioned here, namely, the way in which the overseas commerce was regulated by confining each merchant to a fixed 'stint'. During the first three years he was restricted to selling 100 cloths each year, in the fourth year 150 cloths, in the fifth year 200 cloths, and so on until after fifteen years he was allowed to sell 1,000 cloths. One of the chief objects of imposing these export quotas was, of course, to avoid flooding the market and so lowering the price. This was a restrictive practice of a kind widely practised in medieval times; and by no means unknown today, when groups of manufacturers enter into agreements for limiting production and maintaining prices at artificially high levels.

VI

The Merchant Adventurers, as we have seen, scored an outstanding victory over their ancient trading rivals the Hanseatic League when, in 1567, they entered into a Concordat with Hamburg, the German city that had joined with its near-neighbour Lübeck in founding the League three hundred years earlier. Undoubtedly the English traders had won a battle but not yet, as it turned out, the war, which continued to be waged with the same ruthless intensity as before. In fact, the struggle went on for another fifty years—fortune swaying first to one side then to the other.

One of the retaliatory steps taken by the Hansards was to bring pressure to bear on Hamburg, with a view to having the

Merchant Adventurers expelled; if not immediately then at the expiration of the ten-year period. In that the League was, at least temporarily, successful, for the Company was obliged to withdraw from Hamburg and return to Emden—which had many disadvantages, but was on German soil. By 1580 they were firmly settled at Emden, but the League pursued them relentlessly and, Emden being within the jurisdiction of the Holy Roman Empire, they approached the Diet at Augsburg with the demand that their hated rivals should be banished. Two years later the Count of Friesland was ordered by the Emperor Rudolf II to turn the Merchant Adventurers out of Emden, on the ground that they were trying 'to gather the entire cloth-trade into their hands'. However, Emden was in no mood to suffer heavy losses for the sake of principle. The decree was, therefore, ignored and later set aside.

For five years the Merchant Adventurers remained in the imperial city just across the border from Holland, but again found it unsatisfactory as a trading centre. In 1587 they moved to Stade, near Hamburg, but were able to retain a foothold in Middleburg, on the Dutch island of Walcheren, where they were allowed to enjoy some of their former privileges. The harassments of the League, however, were never relaxed. It made further representations to the Emperor, who in turn wrote to Queen Elizabeth denouncing the Merchant Adventurers as a fellowship of greedy monopolists, bent on 'dispossessing the League of its inheritance of trade'. When, in 1596, the Queen ordered the confiscation of several Hanseatic vessels which had been trading to Spain, the Emperor's patience was exhausted, and in the following year he issued a decree banishing the Merchant Adventurers from German territory. Their position then became extremely vulnerable, for they were surrounded by enemies, ranged against them being the combined opposition of the Empire, the Hanseatic League, and Spain—which despite the destruction of the Armada in 1588 continued to be a powerful military and political force.

Elizabeth and her ministers responded to the Emperor Rudolf's decree by ordering the Hanseatic merchants out of the realm and closing down their London *Stahlhof*, as already related.

VII

The Queen, who had been such a redoubtable champion of the Merchant Adventurers, died in 1603, and was succeeded by James I, whom the wily Hansards thought could be persuaded to reverse her harsh decisions. They appealed for the restoration of their ancient monopoly in London; but without success, for James favoured the trend towards freer and more competitive forms of trading. The Hansards were not, at that time, allowed to return to the Steelyard, which had been converted into a naval storehouse, though an accommodation was reached with them later.

Their power, after three hundred years, was in eclipse. They had entered into an entirely new era and were living in a world whose boundaries had been infinitely enlarged by the discoveries of Columbus, Vasco da Gama and other navigators. Trade was flowing into other channels, passing them by, leaving them stranded. Even in Europe they were losing control over their traditional markets for, despite the interdicts and prohibitions, the Merchant Adventurers continued trading at Stade and elsewhere on the Continent, and with so much success that once again the frustrated Hanse merchants petitioned the Emperor to rectify their grievances. The protest he sent to King James had only one positive result: a conference was arranged in the hope that the ancient enmity between the two great trading groups could be buried and forgotten.

That was in 1610. In the following year Hamburg, by inviting the Merchant Adventurers to go back, dealt yet another blow to the dwindling power and prestige of the Hanse merchants, though they were allowed to return to their London Steelyard, with certain fiscal and other privileges, but not on anything like the former scale. The Merchant Adventurers, on the other hand, were given a fresh lease of life; for their association with Hamburg, a great city which had been founded by Charlemagne in the ninth century, proved to be of an enduring nature. In fact, the Merchant Adventurers eventually became known as the 'Hamburg Company', because of the magnitude of their trade with that city. The development must have been particularly galling for the Hanseatic League, since Hamburg had been one of their most important and loyal citadels. Now, at the moment of crisis, it turned traitor and opened its gates to the foe. The star of the Hanse merchants, as even the least expert astrologer must have seen, was about to set.

They struggled on for another fifty years—until, in fact, 1669 when their last general assembly was held, with only nine towns represented. An event that decisively broke the power of the Hanseatic League was the Thirty Years' War (1618–1648), ruthlessly fought by armies of mercenaries, who left the greater part of Germany devastated. A disastrous war between Denmark and Sweden completed the process of disintegration and left the League no alternative but to dissolve.

VIII

Victory was clearly with the Merchant Adventurers, for after 1611 they had two recognised mart towns abroad—one in Germany, permanent and fixed, and another in the Netherlands, which tended to move about. The Dutch merchants by arbitrary laws, impositions and trickery, forced their English rivals, whose privileges and success they envied, to change their residence with monotonous regularity. From Middleburg, which they did not like anyway, they removed in 1621 to Delft, in 1635 to Rotterdam, and finally, in 1655, to Dordrecht, where a more or less permanent seat was established and they were well treated.

Although the main trade of the Merchant Adventurers was the unfinished cloth so greatly in demand on the Continent, they exported a great variety of other goods—among them corn, beer, leather, lead and tin. The imports were equally varied and included such items as flax, hemp, wax, pitch, tar, timber, wines, drugs and spices, tapestries and linen. Some were basic raw materials, needed to keep the shipbuilding and other industries going, others were pure luxuries.

Essential as the Merchant Adventurers were to the economic well-being of England they were not numerically very strong. Secretary Wheeler estimated that early in the seventeenth century the Fellowship consisted of no more than 3,500 members; but there was a slow, steady increase until about 1650, by which time the numbers had approximately doubled. Most of the adventurers were London merchants actively engaged in trade. A fair-sized minority, however, were content to be 'sleeping partners', or to busy themselves in the administration and direction of the Company's affairs. Matters, eventually, reached the point where it could be truthfully alleged by critics, of whom there were not a few, that 'government of the Fellowship rested in the hands of a small caucus of fifty men, many of them possessed of huge fortunes', and, it may be added, of autocratic dispositions.

The prosperity enjoyed by the Merchant Adventurers, no less than their traditional privileges, brought a new set of enemies into being. At the end of the sixteenth century, in 1598, the Hanseatic League had been dealt a mortal blow when their Steelyard on the left bank of the Thames had been closed. Now the same stalwarts who had forced that issue attacked the Fellowship, which it was held enjoyed far too many official favours. They railed against the monopoly, the restrictions on trade it imposed, and the unfair advantages it conferred. These men, many of them merchants from the outports, openly flouted the Company's charter and set themselves up as free traders.

IX

They had probably always been something of a problem, for the spirit of free enterprise was as irrepressible then as today. As far back as 1613 the Merchant Adventurers had complained to the Dutch that the town of Amsterdam, by encouraging and sustaining the English interlopers was 'draining away their very heart's blood.' Legally, of course, the Company's case was incontrovertible; nevertheless, there were good and weighty arguments on the other side, and these were widely aired. In 1604, the House of Commons itself considered a report on free trade, and it soon became clear that the climate of opinion was changing.

On behalf of the Company it was urged that a 'well-ordered trade', with few but regular sailings in convoy, the restriction of sales to the mart towns, and the selling by wholesale rather than by 'petty retailing in every port and creek of the Continent' was of benefit to every one concerned. It prevented cutthroat competition, kept prices at levels where they provided reasonable returns, and maintained the dignity of the adventurers who chose to regard themselves as merchant-princes and members of a skilled profession. To adopt the methods of the 'rambling pedlars and petty shopkeepers' could, in their opinion, only result in disaster.

Undoubtedly the Merchant Adventurers had been responsible for pioneering and organising an important sector of English trade. By defeating the Hanseatic League they had achieved the status of a great national institution which, animated as it admittedly was by mercenary aims, had yet rendered the country innumerable services. The Company could expatiate on the important part it had played in advancing the arts of shipbuilding and navigation; in training large numbers of shipmasters and seamen—both ships and men being available in times of national emergency. They could claim, without fear of contradiction, that their purses had been open to monarchs in times of war and peace; that they had on several occasions made loans to the Crown and pledged their credit to raise loans for it abroad. They had, by insisting on the use of specially-chartered ships and exercising a strict control over their officials, assisted the Customs in preventing evasions and frauds. With justifiable pride they could draw attention to the chapels they had founded, to the donations they made to charities, to the university scholarship they had endowed, to the native manufactures they sustained by being always willing to buy, even when times were bad. Finally, they did not fail to remind their denigrators of the very important fact that, by their manipulations of the foreign exchanges, they had delayed the sailing of the Spanish Armada for a whole year.

The interlopers' case had been cogently and forcibly put to Members of Parliament in 1604, in the famous *Report on Free Trade*. The crux of their argument was that the Merchant Adventurers had abused their monopoly by exorbitant levies, by striking hard bargains and concentrating the export of cloth, a staple commodity, into comparatively few hands.

1. Queen Elizabeth I, by an unknown artist.
   (*National Portrait Gallery*)

2. Queen Victoria, by Lady Abercromby.
   (*National Portrait Gallery*)

3. Colonists landing in Virginia. (*Mansell Collection*)

4. The fortified village of Pomejooc in Virginia, by De Bry, 1590.

(*Mansell Collection*)

5. Charter of the Hudson's Bay Company.

6. Sketch of Upper Fort Garry, by H. J. Warre, 1846.

(By courtesy of the Governor and Committee of the Hudson's Bay Company)

7. Fort George, Madras. (*Mansell Collection*)

8. East India Whar
London Bridge, b
Peter Monamy.

(*Mansell Collection*)

Prominent among the opponents of the Company were the West Country merchants, especially those of Exeter, who pressed this charge—that the Merchant Adventurers were a 'fraternity of engrossers', i.e. monopolists, intent on keeping all but a favoured few out of the export trade—with pertinacity and vigour. Great mischiefs, it was alleged, were wrought by this virtual stranglehold on trade, not least among the clothiers, or makers of cloth, who, in the absence of other outlets were forced to accept such terms and conditions as the Company thought fit to offer. By plotting and scheming among themselves the adventurers arranged things 'so that they could buy at whatever time, quantity and price they chose'.

In support of the argument for freer forms of trade—and the interlopers were not wild men who wanted it thrown open to all and sundry—it was claimed that they would equalize the distribution of wealth in the realm, and give the provinces a better chance to develop their industries and trade. London, as they pointed out, was not the whole country. 'England's well-being and stability depended not on the riches of a few but of many subjects'. Further, it was maintained that the open trade of the interlopers, and not the closed system of the Merchant Adventurers, produced the best mariners and ships. Finally, the interlopers declared that many buyers at home would increase the income of the clothiers, and that given free trade 'many active and industrious spirits would seek out fresh markets', make quicker returns, and sell cloth in greater quantities. Monopoly might have been a necessary thing when the export trade in cloth was in its infancy; but in the days of James I, when the trade was matured, monopoly, and all the exactions and restrictions associated with it, was clearly out of date.

The struggle went on for several decades—monopoly versus free trade, the provinces versus London, and both sides marshalled and deployed their forces with resolution and skill. What the outcome was we shall see later.

x

The difficulties that beset the Merchant Adventurers early in the seventeenth century were aggravated during the upheaval of the English Civil War, which turned men's minds from peaceful commerce into political and military channels. The Dutch, taking advantage of the position, rapidly developed their wool and shipping industries and began to sell cloth to their German neighbours. Trade was so much disrupted that the Company could neither buy more cloth from the manufacturers nor pay for cloth already received. Parliament, apprised of these defaults, warned the Merchant Adventurers that unless they relieved the clothiers of their accumulated stocks and met their financial obligations the trade would be thrown open to the interlopers, who were indeed already sailing the seas in considerable force.

However, the Merchant Adventurers, following the example of most other City institutions, gave their support to the Parliamentary cause, and in 1656 were rewarded by having their charters ratified. The trade in cloth, it was decreed, would again be restricted to the mart towns, and the interlopers were, in effect, branded as outlaws and rebels. They exercised such patience as they could, and after the Restoration made representations to the Privy Council, which must have lent a sympathetic ear for the Company's privileges were temporarily suspended.

For a few months in 1662, after the passing of a resolution by the House of Commons and with the 'free consent' of the Company, any merchant who wished to do so was allowed to export cloth to any foreign port, with the exception of Dordrecht and Hamburg, which remained exclusive Company preserves. A Parliamentary committee was then appointed to look into the controversy, and reaching a decision in favour of the Merchant Adventurers, free trade was brought to an end. Only four years later, however, after the Merchant Adventurers' trade had been disorganized by the Plague and their offices burnt down in the Great Fire, the interlopers were again granted the freedom for which they had fought so tenaciously.

Still the battle was not over. The Merchant Adventurers, emulating the tactics of their old enemies the Hansards, fought on with every means at their disposal, and in 1683 had the satisfaction of being restored to all their former privileges.

XI

Five years later, in 1688, came the 'Glorious Revolution' which deposed James II and placed William of Orange and his wife Mary on the English throne. For the Merchant Adventurers the event marked a decisive turning point in their struggle against the interlopers, who were able to persuade Parliament that the name by which the Company had become so well-known was no longer deserved, 'the hazards being so small and their voyages so short', and that their privileges were outdated. In 1689 an Act was passed 'for the better encouragement of the manufacturers as well as the growth of wool', and this made it permissible for anyone to export cloth to any part of the world, with the proviso that four companies only—i.e. the Levant, the Eastland, the Russia and the African—would have their monopolies preserved.

That, for the Merchant Adventurers, was the equivalent of a death sentence. Deprived of their monopoly and ancient privileges they were then exposed to the icy blasts of competition from the London, York, Newcastle, Hull, Bristol, Ipswich and other free traders. Jostled, too, by the other overseas trading companies, they were left to play only a minor role in the unfolding industrial, commercial, and political drama of the eighteenth century.

Nevertheless, the Merchant Adventurers, if only because of their expertise in regard to the Continental markets, managed to survive and hold their own for many years. Their corporate knowledge, experience and standing with merchants in the Netherlands and Germany still gave them many advantages over their rivals. The mart towns were still theirs, and here they continued to enjoy their accustomed privileges. Dordrecht continued to give them an honoured position until well into the eighteenth century.

Their principal residence, however, was at Hamburg, the ancient Hanseatic stronghold on the river Elbe, still one of Germany's major seaports. The city, which had escaped the ravages of the Thirty Years' War, continued to allow the Merchant Adventurers many special privileges and, especially after the disbandment of the League, absorbed considerable quantities of English cloth and other manufactured goods. The commerce lasted right through to the early years of the nineteenth century—until, in fact, 1807, in which year the city was captured by Napoleonic troops.

The Merchant Adventurers were then forced to abandon their factory and offices; and their unique Fellowship—'a great old tree which had borne good fruit in its time, but had gradually become overgrown with moss'—passed out of existence.

* 3 *

Merchants of the Levant

THE first mention of a Company of the Levant occurs in 1567, but it is doubtful whether it actually existed at that date. Richard Hakluyt, in his *Principal Navigations* informs us that a body of adventurers intent on trading to the Levant—which meant in those days trading to Turkey—was granted a charter in 1581, valid for seven years. The society, headed by Sir Edward Osborne, was not to exceed twenty persons in number, and had the right of exclusive trading to the dominions of the Sultan Murad III, to whom Queen Elizabeth I had sent a mission two years earlier. The first voyage having proved successful, the adventurers set about developing the trade on a more extended scale.

A group, consisting of wealthy merchants and financiers, contributed to the capital of £80,000, and Queen Elizabeth herself is said to have contributed, or loaned, at least half of this total, out of the proceeds of captured Spanish treasure. The Company was organised on a joint stock, and not on a regulated, basis—at any rate until the later part of the sixteenth century. By this is meant that the adventurers did not trade individually, in the manner of the Merchant Adventurers, but as a corporation, collectively—or, to use the Elizabethan phrase, 'with a single purse'. However, the organization of the Company does eventually appear to have been changed.

The early years of the Levant Company were extremely prosperous, for it was possible to exchange a variety of English goods for others of Turkish origin in a most favourable ratio. So great, indeed, were the rewards accruing to the adventurers that the Spanish and Venetian merchants, who still claimed to

37

'hold the gorgeous East in fee', were roused to active hostility. Both tried to create difficulties and obstacles—the Spaniards going so far as to threaten to have the straits of Gibraltar closed against the English ships.

When in 1588, the charter granted to the Levant merchants lapsed, it was not immediately renewed, mainly because of the excitements caused by the Armada and the abortive attempt at invasion. Eventually, when the matter did come up for official consideration, certain outside adventurers—who had been adversely affected not only by the war but by the action of the Venetian Republic in restricting English trade in the Adriatic—pressed for admittance to the Levant Company, and successfully carried their point. The old Company was, therefore wound up, a new one was formed, and application made for a fresh charter. Granted in 1592, this new charter was made valid for a period of twelve years.

II

The adventurers on that occasion incorporated themselves under the title of *The Governor and Company of Merchants of the Levant* and were a more numerous group. Fifty-three persons are mentioned in the charter of 1592, and twenty more were offered the option of joining the association. In effect, the Merchants of the Levant and the Merchants of Venice were merged into a single body.

Queen Elizabeth, in granting this second charter, was hopeful that the English merchants, reorganized and unified, would be able to challenge the Venetians more effectively than they had done in the past. Though stipulating that she might at discretion revoke the charter before expiry of the twelve years, she gave the merchants exclusive rights to trade in the dominions of Turkey and Venice—and 'also by land through the countries of the Grand Signior into and from East India, by a route lately discovered'.

By way of countering the obstructive tactics of the Venetians in the Adriatic, Elizabeth prohibited the importation of currants into this country in Venetian ships. This trade therefore, together with the 'wines of Candia'—i.e., Cyprus—

became a monopoly of the Levant Company, and proved to be highly remunerative to the adventurers, even after heavy Customs dues had been paid.

In addition to the wines and currants, the Levant Company imported from Constantinople, Aleppo and Alexandria, a variety of other commodities, including raw silk, mohair, drugs and dyes, cotton-wool and yarn, spices, figs, dates, coffee, and Turkish carpets.

This was the basis on which the Merchants of the Levant, late in the sixteenth century, began to build a trade that attained considerable size, and was of some economic import-ance to this country.

Whether the second Levant Company at its inception cont-inued the practice of the first by having a common stock is not entirely clear. William Harborne, who had been the Company's factor at Constantinople, certainly advanced compelling arguments in favour of 'one joint purse' as heretofore, but the evidence leads rather to the conclusion that by 1595 the Company was operating on a regulated basis, with the members financing their own individual ventures.

III

A few years later, in 1600, we find the Merchants of the Levant involved in a Customs dispute. This arose out of the right exercised by the Company of levying an impost on merchants who were not members but who engaged in the Turkey trade. The dues fell on wines and oils—and also on currants, which were then a modest luxury, consumed in quantity, as peanuts are today, by almost everyone. Con-siderable sums of money were collected from non-members in this way—enough, in fact, to defray the expenses of the Com-pany's Turkish agents. Naturally, this led to an increase in the prices of the commodities, and increases in the cost of living were as unpopular then as they are today. The consumers angrily protested.

Finally, a Customs' officer brought the matter to the notice of the Queen herself, suggesting that the Company was, in effect, levying an import duty, and thus infringing a right that belonged to her alone. Elizabeth, with her Treasury emptied by the struggle against Spain and the crushing of an Irish rebellion, found no difficulty in seeing eye-to-eye with her zealous advisor, and in May 1600 ordered drastic action to be taken.

A fleet of the Levant Company's vessels arrived in the Thames with a huge consignment of wines and the much-esteemed fruits. Unloading of the ships, however, was forbidden until the merchants had paid a newly-imposed tax on the cargoes. Objections to that arbitrary action produced only the imperative reply that, since they would not pay, the charter was cancelled!

Some weeks elapsed before the merchants, bowing to the royal will, offered an annual payment of £4,000; and this was accepted as a 'composition for all charges' other than the normal customs dues. Currants and oils, it was agreed, should be made to contribute a little more to the defence of the realm and to the Queen's finances in general. Amicable relations were restored and so, on 31st December 1600, the Levant Company was granted a new charter.

Its terms were very similar to those of the 1592 charter. There was, however, a new clause which referred to the 'farm', or annual rent, that the merchants were required to pay. This charter, like the previous one, was to last for twelve years, but would become void in the event of the stipulated payments not being made within forty days of falling due.

For two years the merchants honourably met their obligations but then, in 1603, the year of Elizabeth's death (and with £2,000 owing to her), faltered. Declaring bluntly that they could not keep up with the demands any longer, they renounced their patents and disbanded.

IV

The reasons for this surprising action—for instead of relinquishing the charter they might have petitioned for a reduction of the levies—were probably that the trade was in decline. This may have been due, in part, to the competitive activities of the East India Company, which was bringing spices and other commodities to England by way of the Cape route. Moreover, many of the Levant Company's directors had helped to found the East India Company, had heavily invested in its shares, and were therefore more interested in promoting its affairs than those of the company they had left. They allowed their capital and energies to flow into the channel where the highest rewards were to be earned.

Another factor adversely affecting the Levant trade lay in the heavy expenses that had to be borne. For the merchants, in addition to the £4,000 levy and the Customs dues, had to maintain ambassadors and consuls in the middle-east countries with which they traded. To cap these various discouragements to enterprise, the Turks were no longer as friendly as they had formerly been. In the circumstances, it is not surprising that the Company should have decided to dissolve.

Still, there does appear to have been a 'phoney' element in this reckless throwing away of privileges, for which other bodies of merchants were willing to pay handsomely, if there was any question of them being transferable. That the directors of the Levant Company were not entirely without ulterior motive is indicated by their neglect to recall the ambassadors and agents from abroad. So a more plausible explanation of the precipitate action in relinquishing the charter may have been that the Company hoped to exert pressure on the new monarch, James I, believing that he would prove to be more pliable than the Queen who, as a merchant adventurer herself, drove far too hard a bargain.

If such were indeed the secret thoughts of the Governor and his assistants, then they miscalculated badly. James, a Scotsman, was almost as astute as Elizabeth—and certainly not less hard up than she had been. He, too, had a flair for business matters, and threatened to recoup himself for the annual £4,000, which had been lost through the Company relinquishing its charter and its cessation of trading. This unexpected obduracy on the part of the monarch had the desired effect. Once again the Merchants of the Levant prayed for the restoration of their monopoly in currants. This move, made in 1604, leads inevitably to the conclusion that, despite all the outlays and hazards, the Levant trade still provided opportunities and was a fairly profitable one.

The return of the merchants to royal favour was not automatic, for there was now an organized and highly vocal opposition to their petition. Other merchants, hitherto excluded, wanted to join in the trade, and their arguments so far carried the day that, after a fierce dispute, the Company was given back its charter only on condition that it enlarged its ranks.

On the vexed question of the impositions a compromise was reached. The king undertook to collect the duty himself, through the normal machinery of the Customs, and the Company did not again have to pay this as a separate tribute.

December 14th, 1605, saw the sealing by James of this further charter, which was granted in perpetuity.

V

Under the title *The Merchants of England to the Levant Seas*, the adventurers resumed their trading with the dominions of Venice and of the Sultan; and, as a gesture of goodwill, King James decreed that the sum of about £5,000, the estimated taxation for one year on currants and wines, should be advanced to the merchants, in order that they might ingratiate themselves with the potentate, in the Oriental fashion, by giving him a massive gift, or bribe.

This settlement proved highly satisfactory to all concerned and laid foundations that were to endure until the final dissolution of the Company some two hundred years later.

VI

There were, of course, fluctuations in the Levant Company's fortunes. During the 1650s, under the Commonwealth, trade was at a very low ebb. So much had the commerce dwindled by then that there was talk of recalling the ambassador from Constantinople, on the score of expense. To make things even more difficult, there was indiscipline among the factors and agents.

After the Restoration in 1660, an attempt was made to overcome these troubles. A petition was presented to King

Charles for confirmation of the charter, to which were added several clauses aimed at strengthening the directors' authority. One of these new clauses provided that the Company's English employees in the Levant who refused to obey orders could be dealt with as mutineers and sent home for trial. Another clause empowered the directors to administer oaths to factors and ships' captains, to ensure that goods consigned to them, or carried by them, were accurately entered and properly accounted for. The object there was, of course, to check dishonesty and place a curb on private trading.

A more controversial proviso in the new charter, granted on 2nd April 1661, restricted membership to persons who had become freemen of the City of London, except when they happened to enjoy the status of 'noblemen or gentlemen of quality'. This clause was not, apparently, inserted at the instance of the Company, but to appease the Lord Mayor of London and the Common Council, who were perturbed by the refusal of some merchants to take up the freedom and its obligations. Nevertheless, the clause gave rise to much criticism from those whom the restrictions tended to exclude.

The trade revived, and the Company took steps to bring the rebel factors to heel. The 'oath of allegiance' met with some initial hostility at Smyrna, but at Aleppo it seems to have been taken with little protest. Then, with the peculations suppressed and other abuses stamped out, the Company's affairs were soon thriving again.

Sultan Mahomet IV, in 1675, considerably extended the area over which the Levant Company was allowed to operate. Competition was virtually non-existent, for Venice was no longer a dangerous rival. Nor had the Dutch and French traders yet succeeded in making any serious challenge, though they did so later. All these circumstances combined to create favourable conditions for the Merchants of the Levant, many of whom were able, in the 1670s to amass great fortunes.

Towards the end of the decade, however, the prospects became less assured, for the operations of the East India Company were, by then, beginning to constitute a real threat. Already the Levant Company had lost much of its trade in spices. This, however, had never been large; but the East

India Company's imports of raw silk, and of silk merchandise, into this country were a different matter altogether. They could only be viewed with alarm, for, increasing year by year, these shipments could clearly jeopardise the Levant Company's very existence.

At last, in 1680, a complaint was lodged with Parliament, but without effect. No redress having been obtained from the Commons, formal 'allegations of the Turkey Company against the East India Company' were drawn up and placed before the Privy Council in the following year.

VII

Great play was made of the fact that the Levant Company exported to Turkey a variety of English goods amounting in value to as much as £500,000 a year. In exchange for these exports it took the raw silk, grogran yarns, and cotton which 'provided work and bread for thousands of the English poor'. The East India Company, on the other hand, exported very few goods, but took abroad huge quantities of bullion. By its importation of raw silk, and of 'a deceitful sort of raw silk,' it was simultaneously taking away the livelihoods of Englishmen, and 'bringing about an infallible destruction of the Turkey trade'.

The Merchants of the Levant asked the king to grant them permission to right this wrong by sailing their vessels round the Cape of Good Hope to trade in the Red Sea; or alternatively, to have the East India Company dissolved, and reformed in such a way that 'the Turkey Company who, by the encroachment of the East India Company upon them, have lost, or must lose, the greater part of their trade, may have some reparation by partaking of theirs'. The plan involved the creation of an entirely new joint-stock in which the Levant merchants, trading as a regulated company, were to be allowed to take shares.

To this memorial of grievances the East India Company replied that the Indian silks were not only as durable and fine as those from the Levant, but cheaper. Since, moreover, it was usual for them to be re-exported, their effect on the manufacture of silk goods in England was negligible. Sir Josiah

Child, Governor of the East India Company, declared—'The truth of the case at bottom is this: the importation of better and cheaper raw silk from India may probably touch some Turkey merchants' profits at present, though it doth benefit the kingdom and not hinder the exportation of cloth. What then? Must one trade be interrupted because it works upon another? At that rate there would be nothing but confusion in a nation'.

Sir Josiah's words carried weight, and the Levant Company failed to achieve its objects. The Privy Council, as well as Parliament, was on the side of the East India Company, which continued its competitive trading in raw silk unrestrained. When war broke out between Turkey and Austria, the demand in the Levant for English goods, particularly cloth, diminished still further, and by 1686 the trade was again in decay.

Nor were these the only, or worst, troubles—for it was at about this time that the French began to make strenuous efforts to capture the commerce, and, with a Mediterranean port at Marseilles, they had a decided geographical advantage. French companies, enjoying royal patronage, were formed at Carcassonne and elsewhere; and under the guidance of Dutch craftsmen, began to make cloth. Once that they had mastered the techniques of manufacture and were in production, these Companies were encouraged to export by generous Government subsidies.

Their inroads into the Turkish market were heavy and successful. The result was that, on the outbreak of war between France and England in 1689, the Levant Company's activities came near to being ended. Naval convoys had to be provided to ensure safe passage for its ships. On one occasion, in 1693, a great fleet of English and Dutch vessels, some four hundred in number, 'the richest fleet that ever sailed for Turkey', was attacked by the French Navy, and almost completely destroyed. That was, indeed, a catastrophic blow, and when news of it reached the Royal Exchange in London many of the adventurers were seen 'to blanch as if they had received sentence of death'.

The decline in the Company's fortunes was apparent to all. Nevertheless, its existence was not determined there and then. Some business continued to be transacted, and eventually, when the French naval power weakened, the Levant trade recovered, and the merchants even enjoyed brief spells of prosperity. From 1718, however, they were constantly facing difficulties, either at home or abroad, and before the end of the century was reached the Company was clearly a spent force.

VIII

But even after 1795 there were a few hectic periods during which the commerce with Constantinople and the dominions of the Sultans flourished. Lord Nelson was elected an honorary member of the Company in 1801, and the interest of other men, such as Nathaniel M. Rothschild, indicates that hopes of its recovery had by no means been finally abandoned. Alexandria, in Egypt, was one of the centres that actually witnessed a late resurgence of mercantile activities, but it was no more than a temporary flicker. The days of privileged monopoly in trading overseas were nearly over.

The role played by the Levant Company in English history, though neither as important nor as spectacular as that of the East India Company, was nevertheless an essential one. Its wooden sailing ships, braving all the ordinary perils of the seas and the extraordinary risks of corsairs and Barbary pirates, kept England in touch with an area of overflowing material wealth and considerable strategic significance. Though it wrested no empire from the Sultans, as the East India Company did from the Maharajahs, it was the means by which economic and cultural relations were forged with Turkey and the countries of the near East, and maintained over a period of nearly 250 years.

In 1825 the end came, suddenly. At the suggestion of the Foreign Secretary, George Canning, the Levant Company surrendered its charter. The Government then took over the consulates, and the trade was declared free.

* 4 *

The Eastland Company

AS a glance at the map will show, the Baltic is, in effect, an extension of the North Sea, entered by way of the Skagerrak and Kattegat and reaching northwards almost as far as the Arctic Circle. Its coastline, shared by Denmark, Sweden, Germany, Poland, Finland and the U.S.S.R., is over five thousand miles long. It is a shallow, stormy sea, and parts of it are ice-locked and inaccessible to shipping for several months every year. At least twice, in 1658 and 1809, the entire sea was frozen over. Copenhagen, Stockholm, Danzig and Riga are among the towns and settlements to which a well-defined group of English merchants are known to have resorted as far back as the fourteenth century. In 1408 Henry IV granted them a charter.

Even at that time the Baltic trade was of importance, but there are few records of its nature and extent, nor of the activities of the Baltic Company for the ensuing 170 years. The probability is that it did not lead a separate existence for very long, but merged with the Merchant Adventurers—a much larger and more powerful body. Not until the last quarter of the sixteenth century, when the struggle of the English merchants against the Hanseatic League was at a critical stage, were steps taken to give the Baltic Company a new lease of life.

In 1577 a ten-year agreement between Hamburg and the Merchant Adventurers had come to an end and, at the insistance of the League, they were then placed on the same footing as other traders. Queen Elizabeth retaliated by withdrawing the special privileges which the Hanseatic merchants in London had enjoyed. The formation of the Eastland Company in 1579

47

may therefore be seen as part of the war of nerves against the Hanseatic League, and in particular a move to wrest from it at least a share of the Baltic trade.

So far as exports were concerned, the Eastland Company concentrated, as did the Merchant Adventurers, on cloth, which, in the inclement Scandinavian countries, was in good demand and readily saleable. However, unlike the Merchant Adventurers, who dealt mainly in unfinished cloth, the East-land merchants were restricted to the export of cloth that was already dyed and dressed. Their chief imports were materials used in the rapidly-expanding shipbuilding industry—timber (including masts), cordage, hemp, tallow, pitch and tar. Cloth was also exchanged for gold, silver, and other precious metals, and for such luxury goods as furs, which are imported from the Baltic to the present day.

II

The Eastland Company—incorporated by royal charter in 1579 and, like the Merchant Adventurers, a quasi-State organization—consisted of London merchants and financiers. All authority was vested in their hands, to the exclusion and annoyance of the merchants of Hull and Newcastle, who thought that the Baltic trade might reasonably be left to them, if only because of their close geographical proximity to Scandinavia. London, however, carried the day, though the charter expressly provided that the Eastland Company would admit Merchant Adventurers to its ranks—and they, as we have seen, were drawn from both London and the provinces.

It is clear that from the beginnings in 1579 the links between the Merchant Adventurers and the Eastland Company were very close, particularly in the north-country towns, where most of the merchants belonged to both groups, held joint meetings as occasion demanded, and combined forces whenever it seemed that their interests, *vis à vis* the London members, were being overlooked or threatened. The extent to which this interpenetration eventually developed may be gauged from the fact that in York, shortly after the Restoration, out of eighty Eastland merchants two-thirds were actually Merchant

Adventurers or had been apprenticed to Merchant Adventurers. Often enough, the governor of one corporation was deputy-governor of the other.

The two companies were, nevertheless, quite separate entities. Both were regulated companies, in which each merchant provided his own capital. Each had its own charter, its own precisely-defined objects, sphere of influence and constitution. Admission to the Eastland Company was open to all merchants of repute who had been in trade at home and abroad for a period of not less than three years. Manufacturers, retailers and persons engaged in handicrafts were specifically excluded, and those who were actually admitted as members had to sell goods in not less than certain minimum quantities. An admission fee or 'fine' of £20—the equivalent of £2,000 today—was payable by all except the sons and apprentices of members, who were admitted free.

The Eastland Company, like the Merchant Adventurers, was ruled over by a small caucus of wealthy London merchants who, once they had achieved office, were not easily dislodged. All policy decisions were made by this body, which consisted of a Governor, a Deputy-Governor and a number of assistants. These men administered the affairs of the Company, made its bye-laws, and appointed its officials. Holding themselves aloof from the common membership they ruled in true oligarchic fashion by promulgating decrees against which there was virtually no appeal. To preserve this autocratic power, a clause had been inserted in the Company ordinances which, in effect, barred members assembled in general meeting from exercising the right to vote.

On most other matters the Eastland merchants modelled themselves on 'Big Brother', the Merchant Adventurers' Company; they had similar rules for apprentices, for the admission of members, for the maintenance of ethical standards in regard to the quality of the goods they sold and their general dealings with customers, for the preservation of amicable relations among themselves, for the reference of disputes to arbitration, and for restraint on private trading.

The Eastland Company also followed the example of the Merchant Adventurers in chartering ships and in appointing certain dates, which had to be strictly adhered to, for despatch of cloth abroad. Shipmasters were under orders to carry only the goods of freemen, and to make true payment of Danish, Prussian and Polish tolls. On the other hand, they had instructions governing the granting of credit to their customers in the Baltic, who were required to pay one-third down and the balance not more than six months later, against bills-of-exchange.

III

Queen Elizabeth's charter of 1579 allowed the Eastland Company, with certain reservations, to trade in all the Baltic countries. The area as a whole had formerly been completely dominated by the Hanseatic League, whose principal centre had been Lübeck, now a West German port. The League was then gradually sinking into a state of decline. Gone were the days when it could bring the English monarch Henry IV to his knees, or defy the Russian Czar Ivan the Terrible, or blackmail the civic authorities of the Hanse towns into accepting its extortions by the threat of expulsion, followed by slow economic strangulation and death. Tho old, medieval order was changing fast.

Ever since Martin Luther had started the Reformation in 1517, the Hansards had been in difficulties. They had seen the whole of northern Europe abandon Catholicism and turn Protestant; they had noted, with alarm, the new political alignments, the shifts of power and, above all, the changing and adverse patterns of trade. After the great religious upheaval there had, for example, been a sharp drop in the demand for wax candles and for the Baltic herrings which had previously been consumed in quantity on fast days. Both wax and herrings had been among League stock-in-trade. Indeed, the humble herring and the herring fisheries had been responsible for the founding of the League in the first instance, three hundred years earlier!

Notwithstanding the waning power of the Hanseatic League it remained, until the late sixteenth century, a force to be reckoned with, and the Eastland merchants when they first visited Scandinavia must have met with stiff opposition.

They made their voyages in the same diminutive sailing ships that in 1553 had taken Sir Hugh Willoughby and Richard Chancellor to Russia by way of the North Cape, and Sir Francis Drake in 1578-80 on a circumnavigation of the globe. They avoided the depths of winter when, more often than not, the harbours were frozen over. Their first foreign residence was at Danzig, but when the burghers deprived them of their privileges and imposed heavier duties they moved to Elbing—then, *circa* 1622, back to Danzig, at that time a Prussian seaport.

Cloth already dressed, was the Eastland Company's principal export. From their staple in the Baltic they traded to Norway, Sweden, Poland and Eastern Pomerania, selling—in addition to cloth—coal, lead and tin. Denmark was a market they had to share with the Merchant Adventurers, though Copenhagen, the capital, seems to have been reckoned as theirs to exploit—as also Helsingör, or Elsinore, on Denmark's north-east coast. Shakespeare made it the scene of his great tragedy *Hamlet* though, so far as we know, he had never been there. Is it too fanciful to suppose that he had heard Eastland merchants talking about it over the winecups in the *Mermaid*, or some other London tavern?

Though, in total value, the Eastland exports from England were considerable they were only a fraction, certainly not more than a quarter, of the Merchant Adventurers' trade.

In return for their good English cloth the Eastland merchants accepted foreign coin, provided it was of gold or silver, corn flax, linen and the essential shipbuilding materials—timber, hemp, cordage, pitch and tar—already referred to above.

IV

Several factors combined to make the career of the Eastland Company a difficult one. Not least among the problems with which they had to contend was the fact, brought to the notice of the Privy Council in 1615, that English merchant ships were not as well-designed, as economic to operate, or as fast as the ships of other nations. Great strides had been made throughout the Tudor period in shipbuilding, and many technical improvements had been made in the structure of sailing ships.

Henry VIII, by building a great warship, the *Grâce á Dieu* of 1,000 tons burthen, had led and encouraged the advance. Yet for many years afterwards the Navy had, in times of war, to depend on merchant-ships, and these, excellent as they were, did not quite reach Dutch or Flemish standards.

The Eastland Company was consequently handicapped from the start, because its higher freight-costs had to be reflected in higher prices for its cloth. The Dutch traders, therefore, had little difficulty in capturing a large share of the Baltic trade. They gained a further advantage by securing heavy discounts on such Scandinavian raw materials and commodities as they required in return for ready cash. Yet another way in which they out-manoeuvred the Eastland merchants was by transporting to the cold, grey lands of the north not only cloth but a variety of produce from the warm south—wines, olive-oil, grapes and other seasonal fruits. No wonder then that the Dutch, with their superior ships, carried all before them in the Baltic—or that the Eastland Company should see its trade dwindling to a half, even a quarter, of what it once had been.

So serious did these difficulties become that the Eastland merchants decided to charter some of the swifter and more adaptable foreign ships. That proposal, however, met with a stern rebuff, because it ran counter to the official policy that all goods, whether exported or imported, should be carried in English ships. For thirty years or more that prohibition remained in force, but was probably more honoured in the breach than the observance. That foreign ships continued carrying cargoes from the Baltic to English ports is clear from a petition of the Eastland merchants at Danzig, addressed to London in the Commonwealth period, asking for a reimposition of the ban.

Their grievances were removed, insofar as the Government was able to remove them, by the Navigation Act of 1651, which, *inter alia*, prohibited the importation into England of any commodity grown or manufactured in Europe except in ships belonging to English owners, or in ships belonging to owners of the country or place in which the commodity was grown, manufactured or produced. The Act was aimed primarily at the Dutch, who virtually controlled the carrying trade. Unfortunately this leglislation, well-intentioned and important though it was, left so many loopholes, provided for so many exceptions, and was in general so unpopular and widely-evaded that the Eastland Company's position remained unaltered. Particularly frustrating for its members must have been the ruling, given in 1653, that naval stores and shipbuilding materials could be imported into England from any port and in any ship!

Another, though comparatively minor, handicap under which the Eastland Company had to operate lay in the fact that their hunting grounds in the Baltic could only be reached by way of the Sound, the narrow channel separating Denmark from Sweden—thirty miles long and at its narrowest point only three miles wide. This highly strategic waterway was controlled in the mid-seventeenth century by the Danes, who did not fail to exploit their geographical advantage to the full. Every ship that passed within sight of the battlements of Kronborg Castle at Elsinore was forced to pay a toll. In Elizabethan times this had been reasonably light, but the Danes gradually raised their demands to the point where as much as £200 would have to be paid before a merchant vessel was allowed to proceed on its voyage. So greatly were the merchants incensed, not only by the amount of the toll but by its arbitrariness, that they forced James I to register their objections in the strongest possible terms with the Danish king Christian IV.

V

During the Interregnum, the Eastland Company saw the Hanseatic League entering into the twilight stage of its long career. All that remained of it after the Treaty of Westphalia had been signed in 1648 were three German cities, and its competitive power was manifestly broken. Any satisfaction that the Eastland merchants may have felt was, however, short-lived, for they had to face fresh troubles—this time at home and against their English rivals. Oliver Cromwell looked on the Eastland Company, as indeed on all other companies incorporated by royal charter, with a somewhat jaundiced eye. He suspended its charter, and allowed the younger generation of merchants, who were free traders almost to a man, considerable licence—not only in publicly proclaiming their views but in despatching their ships to the Baltic with cargoes of cut-price cloth.

The Eastland men threw up their hands in horror at this display of republican arrogance. Realizing, however, that the tide was temporarily flowing against them they bided their time, addressing petitions to the council of State from time to time, in the hope that the new rulers of England might yet have a change of heart and restore their privileges. Like the Merchant Adventurers when under fire from their critics, they tried to touch the conscience of the nation by reminding it of the great services they had rendered, by exporting English cloth to the Baltic countries, by building up and maintaining a fleet of two hundred sailing ships, by providing a nursery for the training of seamen, by helping to fight the North Sea pirates, and so on. No doubt there was a lot of truth in what they said, but their reproaches were in vain.

In the eyes of the Commonwealth leaders, the Eastland merchants were a suspect corporation, unimportant and expendable, who had done well out of the monopoly that a succession of misguided monarchs had conferred on them, but which it was the bounden duty of the Commonwealth, with its vision of a more democratic form of society, to abrogate. So, for more than a decade, the Eastland Company had to keep going as best it could, without official support or even legal status, until at last, with the Restoration, the storm clouds over its head dispersed and the sun shone through.

VI

King Charles II, in 1661, renewed the charter, and the Eastland Company, in more propitious circumstances, might then have entered into a new and more affluent era. Alas, the final Royalist triumph over the Roundheads had little impact on the Baltic trade which, if anything, took a turn for the worse—though there was still, no doubt, some profit in it.

Alien ships, including many owned by the merchants of Danzig, sailed up the Thames with cargoes of goods from Scandinavia and East Germany in such numbers that the

Company, in 1671, urgently appealed to the king to put a stop to the traffic. The petition was referred to the Council of Trade, which was at first inclined to side with the Company, but later took an unsympathetic view when the directors expressed reluctance to comply with certain conditions. One of those conditions was that they should facilitate the admission of new members by reducing the admission fines. Another was that the Navigation Act should be strictly observed and that the Company should make no use of foreign ships. There were also differences regarding the levying of imposts on English exports.

The result of the Company's equivocal attitude was that Sir George Downing—soldier, politician and a Commissioner of Customs—persuaded the House of Commons to pass the Act of 1673, which threw open the trade to Norway, Denmark and Sweden, and forced the Eastland Company to admit all comers to membership on payment of a nominal fine of forty shillings. Parliament thus deprived the Eastland merchants of their charter rights in the western part of the Baltic, but the eastern part of it was recognized as exclusively theirs.

VII

For yet another fifteen years the Company struggled on, and once again, after the Revolution of 1688, it had to face its adversaries, who thought they could now deliver the *coup de grâce*. They pressed home their attack with considerable gusto but did not quite succeed in achieving their object. An Act of 1689, passed for 'the better encouragement of the growth and manufacture of wool', provided that anyone could export cloth to any part of the world, but contained a clause which reserved the monopoly of the Eastland Company in such Baltic markets as it still retained. The London directors were jubilant and thought that this recognition of the Company by Parliament presaged a calmer and more prosperous future.

Their rejoicings were premature, for the market on the east side of the Baltic was too narrow, while elsewhere the competition of other English traders was too strong, to ensure any lasting prosperity. The Company gradually withered away, losing support first in the outports then in London itself until, in 1764, it could be recorded that 'it existed in name only'. The merchants conducted no business, but still, it seems, maintained some kind of corporate existence, electing officials annually and holding meetings of a purely social kind.

The Eastland Company ended with a whimper rather than a bang. But the Baltic trade continued to be of importance —particularly the imports of tallow, hemp and hides, and it is interesting to recall that one of the first of the many Coffee Houses established in London was called the *Baltic*, because its frequenters were merchants with a common interest in the Baltic countries. This famous Coffee House, which stood on the site now occupied by the General Post Office, served as a meeting place for many years—until, in fact, its habitués had become so numerous that ampler and more convenient accommodation became an urgent necessity. They then left and founded their own Baltic Exchange, which still exists and remains an active centre of commerce, though the principal commodity now dealt in is grain.

* 5 *

Traders to Muscovy

THE story of trade between Britain and Russia commences in the reign of Henry VIII, in 1527, when this monarch was pressed to take the initiative in the discovery of the 'north-east passage'. Portuguese navigators, it was pointed out to him, had charted a way round the Cape of Good Hope to the East Indies, while the Spaniards had discovered a New World in the west. Geographical propinquity, no less than national prestige, demanded that England should locate the unknown lands in the far north.

Henry died in 1547 without having done anything, and it was not until 1553, during the brief reign of Edward VI, that the necessary steps were taken to equip an expedition to seek out this northern part of the globe. In that year three small ships were despatched, two under the command of Sir Hugh Willoughby, and one under Richard Chancellor—all three having been equipped at a cost of £6,000 by a group of London adventurers.

The voyage was a stormy one. Willoughby's ships were frozen in the ice and lost with all hands. But Chancellor arrived safely in the White Sea, the first Englishman to have ventured into those inhospitable regions. He was a friend of Sir Henry Sidney, the father of Sir Philip Sidney, who had recommended him to the adventurers, in the warmest terms, as a seafaring man of sound commonsense; and the welcome extended to him by the Russians appears to have been exceptionally cordial. Leaving his ship, the *Bonaventure*, to winter near what is now Archangel, he travelled overland to Moscow, and was invited to the court.

57

Ivan—crowned as the first Czar of Russia in 1547, and later to be known as 'The Terrible'—was impressed by Chancellor, with his lively temperament and wit, and not only entertained him well, but made him the bearer of a letter to King Edward, which promised every encouragement to the London merchants in the development of a mutual trade.

Having given Richard Hakluyt an account of the conditions in Muscovy, and of the barbaric splendours of the Czar's court later to be published in the famous *Navigations*, Chancellor returned to Russia for a second time in 1555, by the same route. In November of that year, he was again in Moscow, entering into negotiations for the exchange of goods that had been envisaged in the earlier discussions.

He left Moscow in the summer of 1556, to report back to the London adventurers, but the *Bonaventure* was, on this occasion, overtaken by disaster. She ran into a storm, was washed up on the dour coast of Aberdeen, and Chancellor, the 'discoverer of Russia', perished with his crew in the angry seas.

II

The group which had equipped the first voyage of three vessels, naturally, suffered a heavy loss, but there was much consolation in the fact that they had been granted a royal charter of incorporation, joining them 'in perpetual fellowship and communalite', and giving them exclusive rights to the Russian trade.

The 'Marchant Adventurers of England for the Discovery of Lands, Territories, Isles, Dominions and Seignories unknown' —to give them their proper title—were further compensated for the loss of their ships by the action of Czar Ivan, who, in 1555, bestowed on them certain privileges, the most important of which were their right to trade in Russia and their total exemption from payment of taxes. Predominant among the reasons for such generous concessions was the fact that Russia, at that time, had no Baltic port, and the shipment of goods, from and into the European market, was carried out under serious handicaps. Everything considered, the auguries were excellent. Russia was not only a vast potential market but a source of valuable raw materials, and so the adventurers' hopes rose high.

Here it is interesting to note that the Russia Company was both the earliest of the English chartered companies to be incorporated, and, so far as can be traced, the first company to be formed on a true joint stock basis.

Sebastian Cabot, who had been appointed the Company's first Governor, was supported in his office, which was for life, by four 'Consuls' and twenty-four assistants. The latter held their positions for one year, and the quorum was fifteen. Endowed with its own corporate existence, as distinct from that of the adventurers, it could sue and be sued under its own name, hold lands and enter into other contractual relationships. Queen Mary's charter proclaimed its right to 'take possession of such territories as might in due course be discovered by the Company or its servants'. Ivan, as already mentioned, executed a formal document which bestowed on the English adventurers the 'free right of entry and of buying and selling throughout his dominions for ever'.

He undertook, *inter alia*, that should any of the adventurers, or employees, of the Company rebel, or commit acts of indiscipline against the chief factor while serving in Russia, to lend all possible aid, including 'prisons and instruments of punishment', in bringing the offenders to book. These agreements having been concluded, the Company commenced operations. Ships, often as many as twelve or fourteen a year, made the voyage to the White Sea, unloading their goods at Rose Island, in the mouth of the Dvina, whence they were distributed inland. Presently, trading centres and 'factories' were opened at Moscow, Novgorod, and at a number of other places.

III

No progress appears to have been made in exploring the north-east passage, or in finding a new route to the China Seas and the East Indian spice islands. There is, however, evidence to suggest that when Elizabeth ascended the throne, in 1558, the trade with the Czar's dominions was quite a flourishing one. For example, the original adventurers had subscribed a capital of no more than £6,000, which comprised 240 shares of £25 each; by 1564 the membership had been obliged to find additional sums amounting to some £42,000, making a total of £48,000, and the shares stood at £200 each.

In exchange for the assortment of English wares, which the adventurers intended to sell at reasonable prices to win confidence, they brought back to these shores a variety of Russian goods. Siberian furs and skins were, of course, a great attraction, but the most substantial imports into England were timber, tallow, oil, wax, and cordage—all of them, at that period, indispensable naval supplies. So high an importance, in fact, was attached to such supplies that instead of bringing the raw hemp to this country, the Company opened works in Russia, and presently found itself enjoying something like a European monopoly in marine stores.

This position, however did not last long, for when the Russians, by capturing Narva, found their way to the Baltic, they were no longer as dependent on Archangel as they had been. As a result, other English traders were able, illegally as it was maintained, to enter the Russia trade, and did so to such purpose that the Muscovy Company was obliged to petition Parliament to step in and call a halt to their depredations.

The interlopers, who included merchants from Newcastle, Boston and Hull, argued that, since Narva was not part of the Czar's dominions as they had appeared on the map at the time that the Company was granted its charter, outsiders were perfectly entitled to do business there, and to use it as a depot.

However, Parliament settled the dispute in favour of the Company, taking the view that the adventurers had risked their capital, besides bearing heavy charges in opening up the trade, and were, therefore, in fairness entitled to their privileges. An Act, unique of its kind, was passed in 1566, which not only confirmed the charter, but in certain respects extended it, as, for example, to include 'Persia and the Caspian Sea', and any other territories that might subsequently be discovered in the north.

Certain rights of joining the Company were granted to the outports but, temporarily at any rate, the London adventurers won the day.

IV

The evils inseparable from monopoly, whether in the fields of home or export trade, then began to manifest themselves, and, only two years after the Parliamentary intervention, we find criticism of the most forthright kind being levelled at the Governor and his court of twenty-four 'staid, discreet, and honest' assistants.

Many of the merchants excluded from the Muscovy Company accused it of covetousness, and this particular condemnation was not only voiced in England, among the would-be-Muscovy traders. In Russia, too, feelings were running high because of the allegedly extortionate prices charged for English goods, which included great quantities of finished cloth, and Ivan, in an outburst of impolite ferocity, described the Company as a breed of 'most greedy cormorants'. And, once again, the 'free traders' ran their ships to Narva, despite the charter, despite Parliament, and despite the armed patrols of the Company, which tried to keep them out by force.

It was a bad time for the adventurers. They suffered a further blow in 1583, for the Dutch merchants began to compete for Russian favours, and the Czar, oriental despot that he was, broke the solemn bond into which he had entered. He declared his dominions open to the merchants of all other countries and, at a blow, the position of the adventurers was undermined. Their trade with Russia withered rapidly.

V

From this point onwards the story of the Company tends to become somewhat involved, and is only to be followed by a close reading of minutes and a study of accounts. All that emerges of interest for today is the fact that an extremely profitable trade with Persia, by the overland route through Russia, was subsequently opened up and carried on for a number of years. Strange as it may seem, the journey, though much longer than through the Mediterranean, was considered safer, though there was at least one reported 'Cossack raid' on the convoys.

From the first expedition some £40,000-worth of Persian wares was obtained, and it appears that during this period, extending from 1566 to 1581, the financial results were by no means unsatisfactory. A little later, however, the Company's affairs were again in decay, and we learn of internal dissensions.

The Governors came and went, the name of the Company was changed several times, and the story is complicated by the operations of a subsidiary which engaged in whale-fishing off the Greenland coasts. We find the adventurers drifting into desperate straits, sued by their creditors, accused of gross juggling of the accounts and intent to defraud. Legal proceedings ended in liquidation of one Muscovy Company and the formation of another. All this is matter for the economic historian, but is far too intricate to be recorded in a brief summary such as this.

The trade with Russia, which had been almost brought to a standstill, was placed on a new footing in 1620, when a treaty was negotiated with the Czar, which reinstated the privileges formerly enjoyed by the English traders. A further ambassador was sent to Russia in 1630, and despite the fact that the House of Lords was conducting an enquiry into the Company's affairs, business prospered and continued to do so for a period of about five years.

VI

The members of the Muscovy Company, according to John Thurloe, secretary to Oliver Cromwell, 'grew very rich and got great estates'. But once again the administrative machinery, unable to cope with its tasks, ground to a halt. Fresh financial difficulties arose; the Governor was imprisoned, and the Company was quoted as an example of bad management and bad finance. A 'Muscovia Reckoning' came to have a highly sinister significance among the sober merchants of the city.

During the time of the Commonwealth, further difficulties

were experienced, for in 1646 the Muscovy Traders had their rights annulled by the Czar, and were expelled—so unceremoniously that they were unable to collect debts due to them before their departure. Among the various explanations advanced for this arbitrary action was one alleging Royalist intrigue at the Russian court. The Czar, it is said, ordered the expulsion of the adventurers and their officials because they were the representatives of a nation which had murdered its king. Diplomatic relations were, for a time, severed.

However, once Cromwell's Government was firmly established, an ambassador, William Prideaux, was despatched to Moscow, and in 1654 the commerce was resumed, though on a less favourable basis than before—all goods imported into Russia being subject to the same rates of duty as were paid by other European countries.

Once again, after the Restoration, efforts were made to recover the exclusive rights which the Muscovy Company had in the past enjoyed, but without success. The market had, by that time, been captured by Dutch merchants, whose commerce with Russia was believed to be forty to fifty times greater than that of their English rivals. King Charles's ambassador returned to London with almost empty hands and, in 1699, the Russia Company ended its career as a joint stock undertaking.

VII

Trade with Russia ceased to be the monopolistic privilege of a small, arrogant caucus of London businessmen, and was thrown open to individual adventurers, prepared to put up their own capital and to equip their own expeditions. They were, however, obliged to become members of the Russia Company, which continued to function on a 'regulated' basis, i.e., as a kind of guild, vested with disciplinary authority. To facilitate entry of these new traders, Parliament passed another Act in 1698, which included the provision that any subject of the realm should have the right to become a freeman of the Russia Company on payment of a £5 fine. With this event the story of the Muscovy Company enters into its final phase. The trade, of course, went on, and in the eighteenth century again reached considerable proportions. This upsurge coincided with the reign of Peter the Great, founder of St Petersburg (now Leningrad), an initiator of Russia's early industrial revolution. He made a tour of Europe, and was particularly impressed by what he saw in Holland and England, in both of which countries he worked in the shipyards as a carpenter. A tablet was erected in Deptford some years ago to commemorate his visit.

That was in 1696, and in the next eighty years English imports from Russia increased until they were nine times greater than they had formerly been, while exports of our own commodities during this period multiplied threefold. One of the most incredible facts is that backward Russia was able to supply us with quite formidable quantities of high-quality iron and steel! On the other hand, the English merchants were reported, in 1762, to be so well established in St Petersburg as to be 'entire masters of the Russian trade'.

VIII

Active as a trading corporation throughout the eighteenth century, we find in the nineteenth that the Russia Company's activities are diminished almost to vanishing point—though as late as 1865 it was apparently making returns to Parliament of certain transactions and dues. At about the same time the meetings of the company were beginning to assume a less business-like character. More and more they tended to transform themselves into convivial gatherings.

Muscovy dinners in London, as a matter of fact, attained the status of important functions, at which it was an honour to be present. According to W. R. Scott, who is one of the leading authorities on the early chartered companies, the Russia Company was still nominally in existence in 1891—at least for social purposes—and as a mere name it survived in the pages of the London Directory to the end of the first decade of the present century.

* 6 *

The Rise, Decline and Fall of
the East India Company

DRAMATIC and colourful as anything in British history, the career of the East India Company began in the autumn of 1599, when a group of London merchants, presided over by the Lord Mayor, held a meeting at which it was decided to form an association for opening up the East India trade.

Quite quickly, the merchants raised £30,000—a very substantial sum for those days—with which to equip a fleet of sailing ships. Queen Elizabeth was then petitioned for a charter, as it was considered that only by means of a joint stock company could a project of such magnitude be successfully kept going. The Queen, by no means averse to a speculative venture of this kind, granted the request, and on 31st December, 1600, the East India Company, destined to play such an important role in the development of the colonial empire, was formally incorporated.

The charter gave the 125 adventurers sole rights in the trade to and from the East Indies, and allowed them the privilege—rare in that age of mercantilism, with its insistence on keeping the bullion reserve intact—of taking from the country a large amount of silver coin, to enable supplies and native commodities to be purchased. This concession was made subject to the condition that the Company was to return an equivalent amount of coin or bullion after each voyage.

II

There had, of course, been trade with the Orient prior to 1600, but it had not been on a large scale. The Levant Company, for example, had approached the Indies by way of the overland route. This, however, had proved long and hazardous: hence the decision of the London merchants to establish, if they could, a direct communication by sea.

Why spices were so important to the Elizabethans is a matter that calls for a few words of explanation. Root-crops were not then available to British farmers who, during the winter months, had little or nothing with which to feed their cattle, with the result that a great slaughter had to take place in the autumn of each year. The meat was salted down in barrels, but salt being another commodity in short supply, its preservation was inclined to be chancy. As the months passed by, the pickled flesh acquired an unpleasant flavour, and it was this that gave rise to the demand for spices.

Those most esteemed were cloves, nutmegs, maces, and pepper, for supplies of which England had for some time depended upon Dutch and Portuguese traders. Because of the large demand all over Europe, these traders had been able to force their prices up to exorbitant levels. This was the decisive, though not the only, reason behind the determination of the English adventurers to seek out the spice islands.

The earliest voyages organized by the East India Company, numbering twelve between 1601 and 1613, were financed separately. A joint stock company of a temporary nature was formed for each enterprise, and when the expeditions returned safely there was a distribution of profits and a return of capital. There were certain advantages in this system of 'terminable' stocks. That it also had disadvantages was only discovered later.

Among the original adventurers was Henry Myddleton, a friend of Sir Walter Raleigh; a Captain Lancaster was in command of the first fleet to set sail. Five tiny vessels, each of about 500 tons burden, completed the ten-thousand mile voyage round the Cape of Good Hope without accident. Lancaster reached the islands, visited Sumatra and Java, captured a Portuguese merchantman, and purchased large quantities of spices. Then, with the holds full, he began the return voyage, and arrived back in London in 1603, to the great joy of the stockholders.

This, the first venture of *The Governor and Company of the Merchants of London trading into the East Indies*, to give them their full title, was crowned with success. Legitimate trade had been combined with an act of lucrative privateering: and it was natural that, after such an auspicious beginning, the adventurers should be eager to reinvest their money in further expeditions.

A second fleet of ships weighed anchor in the Thames in 1604, and although on that occasion one of the ships was lost, the voyage resulted in a substantial profit. A third voyage, undertaken in 1607, yielded the truly magnificent dividend of nearly 300 per cent on the invested capital!

III

Those early successes were, however, followed by occasional reverses. Vessels were lost—one of them with a cargo valued at £70,000 was captured by Breton pirates. Nor were storms and piracy on the high seas the only hazards to be run. Hardly had the Company charted its course to the islands than it encountered a powerful and hostile rival—one, moreover, firmly entrenched at several points. This was the Dutch East India Company, formed in 1602, which, apart from the indisputable fact of prior possession, had strengthened its claims to certain territories and to monopolistic trading rights by concluding pacts with native rulers. The English company was adamant in its refusal to recognize such rights, and maintained that trade in the islands was free and open to all. This clash of trading interests presently affected the relations between the Governments of the two home countries.

Energetic protests from London were countered by equally energetic protests from Amsterdam—for each city stood squarely behind its own traders. There seemed to be no way out of the deadlock until, at last, in 1619 the Dutch signed an agreement in which the English point of view was conceded. Unfortunately, it made little or no difference to the position in the East Indies, for the vendetta between the servants of the two companies continued fierce as ever. On the island of Amboyna, which had been divided between them, the Dutch carried out a raid and arrested a number of Englishmen, ten of whom they executed. This incident, the 'massacre of Amboyna' as it was called,

aroused great indignation in England and was bitterly de-
nounced. Nevertheless, it was clear that the Dutch merchants
were determined to remain masters of the East Indies and to
drive their English rivals out. This, indeed, they were eventually
successful in doing, and the London adventurers were com-
pelled to leave the islands. Their attention was then concentrated on a far richer prize—the vast sub-continent of India,
whose cornucopia of riches was as yet largely untapped by
European traders, though the Portuguese were already
established on the north-west coast. The Dutch, whose East
India Company was virtually a State-owned corporation,
had also found their way to India, and were trying to establish
a permanent foothold there.

IV

At this point an English merchant adventurer of marked
ability and initiative appears upon the scene. William Hawkins,
who left London in August 1608 in a small ship named *Hector*,
had been a servant of the Levant Company, and had not only
become familiar with trading conditions in the Middle East
but had acquired a working knowledge of the Turki language.
He carried with him a letter from King James I to the Indian
Mogul Emperor Jehanghir, requesting the grant of facilities
for mutually profitable trade.

Long-distance voyages in the seventeenth century had many
and varied hazards. Apart from the normal perils of the sea
and of piracy, there existed the danger of contracting diseases
such as malaria, scurvy, and dysentery. Mortality among ships'
crews was consequently always high.

Hawkins, however, survived the ordeal, and in due course
had the pleasure of sighting the western coast of India from the
Hector, which was probably the first English vessel to sail the
Arabian Sea. He reached Surat, destined to be the first British
trading station in India, and went ashore. There the Portuguese
merchants, who were already well established at the mouth of
the Tapti River, opposed him and tried to prevent him
penetrating inland. They even made an attempt on his life, but
failed, and Hawkins, a man of determined character, refused

to be deflected from his purpose. After many adventures, he safely reached Agra—which Baber, the first great Mogul ruler, had made his capital in 1527—and there presented the king's letter.

His reception was of the most cordial kind. The emperor, a man of easy-going temperament, seems to have taken a liking to him, and to have recognised in him a kindred spirit. When it leaked out that Hawkins had a fluent command of Turki, which Jehanghir himself spoke, the English trader's position, *vis à vis* his European rivals, was immeasurably strengthened. Since the services of an interpreter were not required, he was able to have long personal interviews with the emperor, and to press his demands in private.

Those demands could not be lightly or immediately conceded, but as a result of their discussions the two men, despite their differences of race, religion, cultural background, and station, became firm friends. Jehanghir, with the proverbial lavishness of an eastern potentate, appointed the London adventurer honorary commander of five hundred horse, supplied him with money, kept him entertained, and even arranged his marriage to an Armenian girl who was attached to the court.

Despite these marks of the Imperial favour, Hawkins was unable to overcome Portuguese influence with the Mogul, very strong at that time, and he was therefore obliged to leave India with his mission unfulfilled. He took his wife with him, intending to settle down in England, but died on the homebound voyage.

The end was disappointing—yet not completely so. Hawkins had performed a great service for the East India Company: by making his way to Agra, by establishing friendly relations with the Mogul emperor, and preparing the way for other men—Middleton, Thomas Best, and Nicholas Downton—who were to follow and carry the work that he had begun to a successful conclusion. When, in 1612, the Portuguese naval power was destroyed, Jehanghir was pleased to grant permission for an English factory to be established at Surat, and the way was then open for free and unrestricted trade.

Such were the beginnings of a great mercantile empire that was to endure for two-hundred-and-fifty-years.

V

At home, in London, significant events were shaping. The
East India Company, with its charter renewed by James I for
an indefinite period, had been established on firm foundations.
It had obtained a foothold in India; Surat was being developed
as a port, the Company's ships were penetrating as far east as
China and Japan, dividends were being paid, and the future
appeared bright.

Only one shadow, that of the English Civil War, clouded
the deliberations of the court of directors. Hostilities between
Royalists and Roundheads broke out in 1642, when Charles I
raised his standard at Nottingham, and the Battle of Edgehill
was fought. The City was, of course, solidly behind Parliament,
but the Company, constituted as it was by royal charter,
favoured the king. Nevertheless, it did not fail in its contributions to Cromwell's war-chest, and endeavoured, as a corporate
body whose main concern was trade, to keep aloof from the
struggle. After the Royalist defeats at Marston Moor and
Naseby came many anxious moments for the adventurers. In
1649, when Charles was beheaded and a free Commonwealth
proclaimed, the very ground seemed to slip from underneath
their feet—for the charter, and the substantial privileges it
conferred, ceased to have validity. Not even the safe arrival
in the Thames of seven ships, with rich Indian cargoes, could
entirely dispel the air of gloom and despondency that then
descended upon the Company and its affairs. An organization
of rivals, or 'interlopers'—determined, despite the Company's
clear monopoly, to share in the Indian trade—was a further
cause for apprehension.

Certainly the immediate prospects appeared bleak, but hope
revived presently when Cromwell, foreseeing the need for developing English maritime power and intent on establishing
colonies, encouraged the Company in both shipbuilding and
overseas activities. After assuming the title of Protector in
1653, with authoritarian powers, he took up with the Dutch an
issue in which the two Stuart kings, James I and Charles I,
had displayed but little interest. The events at Amboyna in
1623, when the Company's men had been murdered and its

goods confiscated, still rankled, as well they might, for its just claim for compensation had been repeatedly rejected. After Cromwell's intervention, the Dutch paid £85,000—and a further sum of £4,000 for distribution among the relatives of servants who, after torture and the travesty of a trial, had been executed on the island.

VI

This belated settlement with the Dutch gratified the Company but was followed by an event of crucial significance for its future. Cromwell, after his victory in the Civil War, had regarded East India House in the City as a royalist stronghold. Further, he had decided that the charters with their grants of monopoly were a harmful restriction on trade. He therefore allowed other merchants, the interlopers, to engage in the commerce with India and to challenge the Company's position. Eventually, when the smuggling and other evils encouraged by this policy were recognised—and after the directors had delivered an ultimatum—Cromwell's attitude changed. He was forced to grant a new charter.

This reaffirmation of the old privileged position of the East India Company had a remarkably stimulating effect on the stockholders, who subscribed fresh capital to the value of £740,000—half of which was immediately forthcoming—and gave their directors a free hand to plan fresh enterprises in the Mogul territories.

We have already noted how the early voyages were financed separately, a joint stock company of temporary character being formed for each venture. The drawbacks to this method of providing capital were several: it made the accounting more complicated—for the ventures overlapped; it necessitated raising fresh capital for each new project; and it led to competition between the ships—competition, that is to say, for cargoes. Naturally, the arrival of some half-dozen English merchantmen, all keen on buying wares or produce, delighted the Indian traders—because it forced up prices—but the Company, involved in heavy losses, was less pleased.

So, in 1657, a fundamental change was effected: the East

India Company placed its capital on a permanent basis. With large areas of India open for commerce, with fortifications to construct and local defence forces to equip, the step was inevitable. There was urgent need of a stabilized fund on which the directors could draw for purchasing supplies, for shipbuilding, and for development generally. Lacking such a fixed capital it is difficult to see how the Company could have made any progress at all.

Nevertheless, there were critics who debated the point with considerable heat. It was maintained that a 'regulated' company —or an association of individual traders, each supplying his own capital—would serve the national interests better. Attention was drawn by the 'bullionists' to the considerable amounts of treasure that were being shipped abroad—for the Indians were not greatly interested in barter arrangements, i.e., accepting English woollen cloth in exchange for their silks, calicoes, and other goods, but insisted on cash. There was a measure of truth, therefore, in the accusation that the country's economy was being undermined by the removal of precious metals and of specie. Pressure was also exerted by opposition groups of merchants, interested in the highly profitable commerce with India, and these men found much support in their argument that the Indian trade should be open to all.

They had, in fact, done very much as they liked from 1654 to 1657, with Cromwell's full consent. The Company, however, had played a trump card by threatening to withdraw from India and to dispose of its properties there. This sharp ultimatum made the Protector think again, and, being a practical man, it is not surprising that he decided to renew the monopoly which the Company had enjoyed before the Civil War broke out.

VII

The return of the East India Company to official favour was an effective rebuff for the interlopers, and some thirty years were to elapse before they were able to stage another full-scale attack. Prudence suggested that, for the time being, they should bow to superior force and hold their fire. Some of the more astute bought their way into the Company, and joined the court of directors.

In 1658 Cromwell died, and two years later the monarchy was restored. The Company then entered a period of great affluence—for Charles II proved himself its very good friend. The Protector's charter, in turn rendered worthless, was destroyed and forgotten. A new document was issued; not perhaps too regularly—as the king had still to be crowned—and yet valid enough for all practical purposes. This charter empowered the Company to appoint Governors in India, to wage war or conclude peace with native princes; to administer justice; to acquire territories and, most important of all, to seize and send home the ships of interlopers. Four subsequent charters under the seal of Charles II modified, consolidated, and extended the rights of the Company—and so there is no doubt that, after 1660, its star was very much in the ascendant.

Two years after Charles's triumphal return from exile he married Catherine of Braganza, daughter of the king of Portugal—an event not without significance for the East India traders. Included in Catherine's dowry were the Portuguese possessions of Tangier, opposite Gibraltar, and Bombay, an island off India's west coast. For several years Bombay remained a royal possession, but an unprofitable one. Charles therefore handed it over in 1668 to the Company, in return for a loan of £50,000 and a quit rent of £10 a year. Surat then began to decline in importance as a port for English ships.

Throughout the 1660s and the 1670s the Company's affairs continued to prosper. The trade, unspectacular but steady and continuously expanding, was mainly in such commodities as cotton stuffs, Indian silks, saltpetre for the making of gun-powder, coffee and tea. The last mentioned had been introduced into Britain by the Dutch in 1645 and, though expensive at first it gradually became popular. As demand increased, after the Restoration, the Company imported more tea and had, in fact, to construct a special warehouse in London for storing it. This tea did not come from India but from China, where the custom of drinking it dates back to remote antiquity. India's tea industry was not founded until the early part of the eighteenth century.

In 1683 came another trial of strength between the Company and the interlopers, one of whom—a Captain Sandys—had traded with Portuguese Goa without permission asked or given. Since they were now entitled to suppress competitive trading, the directors ordered arrest of the miscreant, who was taken to the President at Surat and made aware of the Company's displeasure. Eventually the law was invoked. The case came up before Judge Jeffreys, notorious for his Bloody Assize after the Monmouth rebellion, and was decided by him in the Company's favour. Once again the attack of the 'anti-monopolists' was beaten off.

In 1685 the clever, cynical and blasé profligate whom we know as the Merry Monarch died, and was succeeded by his brother James, who had in various ways demonstrated that he had the East India Company's interests at heart. Unfortunately, from the directors' point of view, James was destined to occupy the throne for only three years. The Glorious Revolution of 1688 forced him to flee the country, never to return.

Before moving into the next decade, there is one event, of overwhelming importance for the Company and for India, that needs recording. A rival French company *La Compagnie des Indes Orientales*, founded in 1664, had set up its agencies on the Indian coast; at Chandernagore, in west Bengal in 1673, and at Pondicherry ten years later. With the French in India, challenging the English at various points, and with the Mogul Empire showing every sign of breaking up, the stage was set for truly world-shaking events.

Both groups of traders armed themselves, raised fighting forces, intrigued with the native princes, and were soon at one another's throats.

VIII

After the hurried departure to France of James II in 1688, an invitation was extended to William of Orange, who had married James's elder daughter, Mary, and who was a grandson of Charles I, to accept the vacant throne. During his joint reign with Mary, English commerce made a number of dramatic advances. In 1694 the Bank of England was founded, and before the end of the century joint stock companies were active in many diverse fields—manufacture, the public service (as, for example, Dockwra's Penny Post) overseas colonization, and general trading. For the East India Company, then under the able Governorship of Sir Josiah Child, an entirely new era began. A supporter of the Stuart monarchy, Sir Josiah was very much in the black books of the political party then in power—the Whigs, who upheld the hated interlopers in their renewed and insistent clamour for free trade.

They had, in fact, presented a petition to Parliament demanding the right to set up a *second* East India Company, as legal competitor to the one already in being! This petition was given a sympathetic reception, though it was quickly realised in the House of Commons that the old Company was in an exceptionally strong position. All the advantages were on its side; the treaties with the Indian princes, the fortified trading positions at Surat, Bombay, and Madras, the fleets of ships capable of rounding the Cape and carrying worth-while cargoes, the long decades of experience. For these and other reasons Parliament was bound to consider the suggestion for immediate termination of the charter as thoroughly impracticable, and, in any case, the Company was entitled to three months' notice.

The desired end, which innumerable enemies had been unable to encompass, was brought about by a blunder made by the Company's own secretariat. In 1693, because a Government tax, levied on joint stock companies, was paid a day too late the charter was held to have lapsed! It was, of course, a purely technical default, which in other circumstances would have been overlooked. But there it was—the Company had delayed payment until March 25th, forgetful of the fact that the Exchequer was closed on that day, which then ranked as a public holiday.

The error was, of course, gleefully seized upon by the opposition. At last the opportunity had arrived by which its aims, frustrated for so long, might be achieved. Renewing their demands with utmost vigour, the Company's attackers were able to create a sizeable breach in its defences. The charter was, indeed, restored but, taking advantage of the secretarial oversight, the Government was able to impose a number of new conditions.

These included the formation of the second East India Company by the rival group of merchants, who, in appreciation of the Government's action, loaned it a substantial sum of money with which to replenish an exhausted war chest. In 1698 the new Company was formally incorporated, and for some time afterwards *two* East India Companies existed side by side!

However, the dissensions that followed this judgment of Solomon were so violent, and so damaging to the national interest, that, finally, everyone concerned with the India trade agreed that the only sensible course was for the two companies to amalgamate. This they did under the title *United* East India Company in 1709, when Queen Anne was on the throne. Well over a hundred years had passed since the grant to the adventurers of the royal charter which had brought them into corporate being.

IX

Meantime, in India, the Company had, through the initiative of a chief factor named Job Charnock, established itself in a strong position on the river Hooghli, the most westerly of the many mouths of the Ganges, at a point some eighty miles from the sea. Charnock, a somewhat elusive figure, went to India during the Commonwealth period, and at some time after his arrival entered the service of the East India Company. He went to Cossimbazar and to Patna, at both of which places were 'factories' carrying on a chancy trade. Finding the position there untenable, Charnock—without orders from London—moved southwards and, at a small village named Sutanati, set up an encampment which he intended to be no more than a temporary resting place.

Swampy and fever-ridden, the site was decidedly unattractive, but had certain practical advantages: it was well placed for expeditions along two great watercourses, the Ganges and Brahmaputra, and it was militarily defensible. Charnock seems to have altered his mind about the impermanence of his halt at Sutanati—indeed, he formed a stubborn resolve to remain there. When attacked by the Mogul's viceroy he resisted, and, after fluctuating fortunes of war, obtained a grant of the marshy site on which he had planted the Company's flag.

The rude settlement developed at unexpected speed. A stronghold—the 'old' Fort William—was built in 1696, quays and warehouses were constructed, a deep-water harbour was found for the great sailing ships; men and materials arrived from England, and trade flourished. Soon the new port of Calcutta—which is now the capital of Bengal and one of the greatest cities in Asia—was worth more to the East India Company than Bombay and Madras put together. Charnock did not live to see all this, he died in 1693, but the directors in their London courtroom acknowledged the greatness of his accomplishment, and posterity, too, has done so, for Calcutta is admitted to be virtually his creation.

Since the accounts of him are so fragmentary—even the date of his birth is not accurately known—little can be recorded of his personal life. There is, of course, the romantic story of his marriage to a young and beautiful widow who, in compliance with the Hindu custom of suttee, was about to be immolated on her husband's funeral pyre. Charnock, according to the legend, snatched her from the flames, made her his wife, and had several children by her. When she died he buried her in an enclosed piece of ground in the suburbs of Calcutta, on which the Church of St John's now stands, and erected a mausoleum in which he, too, was eventually to be buried.

X

Job Charnock, who served the East India Company faithfully for over thirty years, was followed by other men—young, mettlesome, and daring—whose personalities are still flaming in our history books. Outstanding, of course, was Robert Clive, who began his career at Fort St George, Madras, in 1744, as a 'writer' or clerk. He was then seventeen years of age, a youth of weakly constitution, with no more than the average of ambition or ability. No one, whether in London or Madras, could have had the slightest inkling of the dominant role he was to play in Anglo-Indian affairs.

Clive came to India at a historic turning point. The Portuguese were a spent force, and the Dutch, confining themselves to the Indonesian islands, had ceased to be a threat. But new and more powerful rivals were now upon the scene, determined to make a bid for supremacy on the sub-continent. Mention has already been made of the formation of a French East India Company and the establishment of French trading stations at Chandernagore, in Bengal, and at Pondicherry, on the Coromandel coast. When, towards the middle of the eighteenth century, the Mogul Empire, harried by the warlike Mahrattas of west and central India, looked like foundering, a fierce rivalry developed between the two groups of traders. British and French aligned themselves with opposing native rulers, and soon found themselves locked in a life and death struggle.

Fighting began in 1746, when Joseph Francois Dupleix, who had become Governor-General of French India four years earlier, launched an attack on Madras and drove the English out. Clive escaped, by disguising himself as a native, to a nearby English settlement, Cuddalore, smaller than Madras but well-fortified. The garrison of English and Sepoy soldiers were, at the time, under the command of Major Stringer Lawrence, who organized an East India Company army with which to hit back at the French forces. Clive, having displayed his 'martial disposition' in local engagements, was commissioned as an officer. Warlike actions, aimed at the capture of French Pondicherry were begun, but soon afterwards Britain and France made peace at Aix la Chapelle; there was a lull in the fighting, and Madras was returned.

A somewhat extraordinary situation then arose. Though hostilities between the two home countries had ended they presently flared up again between the contending groups of traders, who were caught up in the tangled web of local events. Delhi's authority over the local princes had almost ceased to exist, and they readily entered into the intrigues of the rival East India Companies, making alliances first with one and then with the other. The overall effect of this crumbling of the

Mogul dynasty, and the state of anarchy that resulted, was to create a power-vacuum which had inevitably to be filled. No doubt the shrewd Europeans on the spot, backed by massive financial resources, by military might of a formidable order, and by strong naval forces, appreciated this. Clive, newly recruited to a military career, suddenly revealed his potential by seizing Arcot, a small town of strategic importance on the Palar River, which the French had used as a major supply centre for themselves and their local allies. Arcot's capture, made after a long march through wild country, and its subsequent defence, were thrilling exploits, the story of which has often been told.

Clive and his few hundred men, most of them Sepoys, resisted a fifty-day siege. Then, aided by the Mahrattas, they engaged the 10,000-strong army of French and Indian besiegers in battle, and emerged victorious. The impetuous young ex-writer certainly distinguished himself in this unequal contest. Besides raising British prestige in the eyes of the wavering Indians, he demonstrated something probably not fully realised till then: that he was a born leader, with daemonic drive, energy and courage, and the ability to weld his men into an almost fanatical fighting unit.

In England, to which he returned for health reasons in 1753, he was acclaimed a national hero.

XI

Arcot, and the subsequent jungle-skirmishing—to say nothing of bad food, a bullet wound, tropical heat and rains—had taken their toll of Clive's constitution, and he was near to collapse. He had married, shortly before leaving India, Margaret Maskelyne, a cultured and beautiful woman with whom he was very happy. For three years he was in England on sick leave; then, rested and refreshed, the East India Company, whose servant he remained, sent him back, with the rank of lieutenant-colonel, to deal with other troubles. With him went a contingent of the King's infantrymen, and some heavy artillery.

On reaching Bombay he went immediately into action

against the west-coast pirates who had for a long time menaced
European shipping. That task successfully completed, he sailed
for Madras, where the Nawab of Bengal, Suraj-ud-Dowlah, in
defiance of Delhi, had seized control of huge tracts of country.
Commander of a big French-trained army, he was hostile to the
English adventurers. In June 1756 news reached Madras that
the Nawab's forces had taken Calcutta, the 'cotton-thread
town' which, since Charnock's day, had grown into a prosperous
trading centre. The occupation was accompanied, as Clive
explained in a letter to the Company in London, by the 'most
barbarous and cruel circumstances to the poor inhabitants'.

At last, after long delays, the Madras Board placed Clive,
fretting with impatience, in charge of an expedition to recapture Calcutta and recover for the Company its lost rights and
privileges. He hoped also to dispossess the French of Chandernagore, twenty miles north of the town, and so strengthen
the English positions. A formidable fleet, including five ships
of the Royal Navy, left Madras and, in December 1756,
entered the Hooghli River. Clive's troops, some European some
Indian, launched an energetic attack, and again, despite the
incredible odds, won the day! The enemy's armoured elephants
turned tail, his 30,000 horses stampeded, and 20,000 foot
soldiers—convinced of the mad, fiery-tempered English commander's invincibility—dispersed in panic. Calcutta was retaken.

When Clive entered the town, he found that the Nawab's
men had, indeed, been guilty of atrocities. The worst was that
of the 'Black Hole of Calcutta' in which 146 British and other
prisoners, including one woman, were involved. Their cell,
measuring eighteen feet by fourteen feet, had only two small
window lights, and conditions rapidly became unbearably hot
and foetid. When the guards opened the doors in the morning
only twenty-three of the prisoners were still alive. This was,
unfortunately, only one of many heedless and inhuman deeds
perpetrated by both sides.

After the defeat of his forces at Calcutta, Suraj-ud-Dowlah
was obliged to observe an uneasy peace. He entered into fresh
intrigues with the French, and on learning that war had
broken out in Europe between France and Britain, prepared
to renew the struggle. He still hoped to outwit Clive, and to

make good his boast that he would drive the whole riff-raff of the East India Company out of his territories and into the sea.

XII

In March 1757, Danton's famous dictum *Toujours de l'audace* had yet to be coined, but the principle appears to have been well understood by Robert Clive, chief protector and advancer of the Company's Indian interests. The war in Europe—which we now refer to as the Seven Years' War—had sharpened the issues between French and English in the Asiatic sub-continent. Clive, making his own swift assessment of the situation, decided to force a decision against his opponents without delay. He struck at Chandernagore, the French settlement to the north, and, supported by men of war which had sailed up-river to silence the French artillery, was able to seize the fortifications. Chandernagore, after a gallant defence, hauled down its flag and surrendered.

The victory was a crucial one, and the alarm of Suraj-ud-Dowlah understandable, for he had backed the French to win, and even now refused to believe that they had suffered anything worse than a temporary setback. In the three months after the capture of Chandernagore—that is to say, between March and June 1757—he made preparations for a crushing counter-stroke, raising an army of 50,000 men, in which were included 15,000 cavalry and a strong French contingent. This force, together with heavy guns and elephants, he put into the field at a place called Plassey, eight miles north of Calcutta, in a position well protected by entrenchments and a bend in the river. Clive's forces, by comparison, were derisory: three thousand men, most of them Sepoys, a few small guns, no cavalry at all. Yet it was Clive who, with a touch of reckless bravado, made the opening moves in one of the most extraordinary battles in history.

Stung into action by this unexpected attack, the Nawab's army emerged from behind its defences and, with supreme confidence in its overwhelming superiority in numbers, swept down on the British lines. To an impartial observer hovering over the plain in a helicopter—had that been possible—it must have appeared that Clive's pitiful battalions were doomed to annihilation. However, the Nawab's 'human sea' was itself highly vulnerable, and when the British guns and muskets opened fire it was with devastating effect. Great holes were torn in the ranks of the advancing army, which came to an abrupt standstill and then, when Clive ordered a bayonet charge, precipitately fled. Everything was abandoned—the dead, the wounded, weapons, equipment, and supplies.

Plassey established British predominance in Bengal, India's richest province, and throughout the peninsula. Dutch, French, and Portuguese influences were eliminated, and the East India Company awoke to the fact that it had an empire to govern. The power that had fallen into the hands of its directors was retained and used to such purpose that, before the end of the eighteenth century, they exercised authority over vast territories, and countless millions of people. The control and commercial exploitation of India became the prerogative of an English joint stock company, inspired by nothing more worthy than the profit motive, and having, so far as the Indians were concerned neither a soul to be damned nor a body to be kicked.

That, shortly after Clive's victory, a number of black pages were written into our history, that bribery, corruption and extortion became rampant, is not surprising. The Company paid its servants badly—Clive as a writer had initially received only £5 a year—and left them to supplement their incomes by private trading and activities 'on the side'. With absolute power in their hands, is it any wonder that the commanders, officers, agents and factors in India should degenerate into greedy tyrants?

When, eventually, rumours of their misdeeds reached the ears of the British public, criticisms began to be voiced. The very clerks and curates, it was alleged, were able after a few years in India to return home rich beyond the dreams of avarice! Before long the whispers had swelled into a storm of denunciation.

XIII

Something must now be said about the more humdrum side of the Company's business. The charter, for example, had come up for consideration several times since the 'London Company' and the 'English Company' had amalgamated under the title of 'United Company' during Queen Anne's reign. Renewals were granted in 1730 and 1744 in consideration of substantial advances to the Governments of the day. The dramatic events in India, of course, converted the Company into a great national institution, abused, as all great institutions are, but also respected and envied. We find the Governor and directors with so much greatness thrust upon them, becoming increasingly conscious of their importance and dignity.

The Company had, in the early part of its existence been content with comparatively modest business premises. In fact it had entirely lacked a settled home of its own, office accommodation having been provided by one of the first Governors —Sir Thomas Smythe, who allowed some rooms in his mansion in Philpot Lane to be used for the purpose. Later, Crosby Hall in Bishopsgate, had been leased from the Earl of Northampton and occupied for seventeen years. Then, when another Governor, Sir Christopher Clitherow, offered accommodation, came the move to a site, bounded on the north by Leadenhall Street, which is very approximately the same as that on which Lloyd's building now stands. There followed, in Commonwealth times, the move to Lord Craven's House, which adjoined Clitherow's but was larger. This building, though in sad repair, had a small frontage on Leadenhall Street, and formed the nucleus of what was to become the Company's permanent headquarters.

Having miraculously survived the Great Fire, additions were made to it in the 1720s when some adjacent properties were purchased. But—converted into a bewildering complex of warehouses, offices, gardens, and yards—it in no way reflected the wealth or standing of Europe's most powerful and successful trading corporation. The directors, recognising this, eventually ordered the old East India House to be pulled down, and commissioned an eminent architect, Theodore Jacobsen, to prepare plans for a new one. Though, when completed, it offered many amenities for the directors and staff which had not previously existed, it still failed to satify those who were most mindful of the Company's rising prestige and status.

At last, after Clive's famous victories in India, it was decided that the London offices should be completely rebuilt. The main alteration made was the extension of the Leadenhall Street façade to an overall length of about two-hundred feet. Architecturally, this new frontage—with its fine portico, its pediment supported by Doric columns, and allegorical sculptures was undeniably impressive. Crowning the splendid edifice, as we can see from old prints, was a figure of Britannia seated on a lion.

Through the stately, neo-classical doorway opening on to Leadenhall Street came and went a stream of officials, directors, captains of East Indiamen, administrators, governors of provinces and agents. The names of most of them are long since forgotten. They did their work, took their pay, and are gone. One of the few still remembered was a clerk in the accountant's department—Charles Lamb who, in his free time, wrote essays.

An amusing description has been left by Thomas de Quincey of the office in which Lamb spent his working life. It was a large yet airless room; six 'quill-driving gentlemen' sat behind a high railing 'all too profoundly immersed in Oriental studies' to notice the presence of a stranger. Lamb sat in an aisle, perched on a very high stool, submerged in 'lofty Leadenhall speculations', but quickly thawed when de Quincey, famous for his *Confessions of an English Opium Eater*, presented a letter of introduction.

Another employee, Thomas Love Peacock, who became head of the Examiner's Department in 1836, achieved great popularity as a novelist. Even more renowned was John Stuart Mill, the economist and philosopher, who entered East India House in 1823, and rose to be Head Examiner of Indian Correspondence before he retired thirty-six years later.

XIV

That, however, is rather anticipating events; for the career of another remarkable man of the eighteenth century has yet to be noticed: Warren Hastings who had, like Robert Clive, gone to India as a writer or clerk. He settled in Calcutta, and there distinguished himself during the Bengal fighting. It was as a result of this that he attracted Clive's attention.

Hastings, a product of Westminster School, enjoyed robust health, and was chiefly remarkable for his administrative and executive abilities. That was far from being a misfortune, since Clive's task in the military sphere having been, to a large extent, accomplished, the pressing need was now for someone with organizing talent to hold the newly-acquired empire together and control it on the Company's behalf. Warren Hastings filled the role to perfection. He became a member of the Calcutta Council in 1761, and was appointed Governor-General of Bengal eleven years later. This title was changed in 1773 to that of Governor-General of India, and in that capacity he exercised immense authority. Unfortunately, like Clive, he was of an autocratic nature, given to acting in a high-handed manner, with the result that he made enemies, and had to face prolonged criticism from Parliament in his later years.

Clive, after the Battle of Plassey, again had to leave India temporarily for health reasons. Having installed a new Nawab, Mir Jaffir, in Bengal, and accepted his extravagant 'gifts', he went home the wealthier by £300,000, to which must be added the quit rent of land in the Calcutta region amounting to £27,000 a year. He was, therefore immensely rich, and on arrival in England at once embarked on lavish expenditure, buying up furnished houses, and anything else that took his fancy. King George gave him an audience; the electors of Shrewsbury returned him to Parliament; in 1762 he was created Baron Clive in the Irish peerage. Pursuing the same masterful tactics that had proved so successful in India, he strove to force his will on the House of Commons, and to overthrow the directors of the East India Company, though he was still, nominally their servant. To strengthen his hand in regard to the directors, he bought £100,000 of stock. But both the Company and Parliament proved exceptionally tough, and he succeeded only in arousing enmity, opposition, and envy.

Clive's third and last visit to India was made in 1765, and during his comparatively short stay of twenty-two months he carried out administrative reforms, and obtained for the East India Company the formal overlordship of Bengal province.

On his return to England the smouldering resentments that had been building up against him broke out in red-hot fury. Enemies of all kinds—personal, business, and political—rushed in to the attack. In 1772 a Parliamentary Enquiry was made into the allegations brought against him of greed, corruption, and oppression. Though he was in the main, acquitted of these charges, the hostility and prejudice against him remained unappeased. His mind gave way; he became depressed, took to opium, and in 1774 committed suicide.

Opinions about Robert Clive have differed—and mention of his name still has power to provoke controversy. His earliest biographer, Charles Caraccioli, who was also his outspoken critic, declared that his victories in India, both military and civil, were due to a combination of good luck and the natural timidity of an effete people. Lord Macaulay, the historian, had this to say: "Clive, like most men who are born with strong passions, committed great faults . . . but our island has scarcely ever produced a man more truly great, either in arms or in council."

To that one can only add that he raised the Company of Elizabethan adventurers to the pinnacle of their greatness.

XV

The Regulating Act of 1773 has importance because of a new principle it introduced, namely the interest of the State in Indian affairs. After the passing of this law the East India Company ceased to be an autonomous body, virtually free to decide issues of war and peace, and to exercise its charter rights regardless of national and international consequences. Dual control, aimed at curbing excesses and establishing a more responsible system of Government over India and its people, came into being. The Act provided for the appointment of a Governor-General, a Council and a Supreme Court; in 1784 there followed Pitt's India Bill, which created a Board of Control, and gave Parliament a voice in all matters relating to India's military, political and financial affairs. Restrictions were placed on the Company's administrative authority.

Warren Hastings, as we have seen, was the man chosen in

1773, when Lord North's Regulating Act was passed, to become the first Governor-General of India, an office for which he was eminently suited. Many difficulties confronted him, however, for the country had yet to be pacified. The feudal system which the Moguls had kept in being for two-hundred years was battered but not broken. The warlike Mahrattas were still active, and it was inevitable that, faced by such complex issues, Hastings should make mistakes and run into trouble.

Two years after he was appointed Governor-General, a native Indian, greatly daring, brought a charge of corruption against him, which charge was of a sufficiently serious nature to make him write home tendering his resignation. As it happened, the Indian, Nand Kumar, was himself shortly afterwards arrested and brought before the Court on a charge of forgery. In view of the altered circumstances Hastings—though aware that London had accepted his resignation—decided to remain in office. Indians were profoundly shocked by this incident, for Kumar, regarded as guilty of only a minor offence, was hanged. To make matters worse, he had been a Brahmin, a member of the Hindu priestly caste, and as such held in high respect.

Some years later Warren Hastings was involved in another damaging affair. He clashed with a fellow-countryman, Sir Philip Francis, who had opposed him in Council and challenged his decisions. This rival the Governor attempted to silence by challenging him to fight a duel. The two men met at 6 a.m. on 17 August 1780, and Hastings proved himself the better shot. Francis, badly wounded, was obliged to return to England, where he took his revenge by providing the evidence against Hastings that was later to be used in the House of Commons with such devastating effect.

The period immediately following the duel was again a critical one in British-Indian affairs. Mysore, the state that lies between Madras and Bombay, had been established by a Hindu dynasty in the fourteenth century, but entered its most prosperous phase four hundred years later, under Hyder Ali, a Mohammedan ruler. Acting in concert with the French, who were again on the offensive, this potentate threatened to nullify the hard-won British gains. Only prompt and resolute action on the part of Warren Hastings saved the situation. By the time that he resigned and sailed for home, in 1785, the conquered regions—Bengal, Oudh, Hyderabad, and the Carnatic—were again securely under his control.

Just as Clive had been attacked, so was Warren Hastings attacked. His actual impeachment, on the grounds of corruption and cruelty during his administration, began in 1788, three years after his return. His trial in Westminster Hall—engineered in part by his old enemy, Philip Francis—was a sensational event that lasted, on and off, for several years. In 1795, despite all the rhetoric of Burke and Sheridan, he was acquitted. The East India Company granted him a pension, and he retired to the seclusion of the Worcestershire estate he had purchased. There he devoted himself to the study of Indian and Far Eastern history, which interested him to the end of his days.

XVI

Pitt's India Bill of 1784 created, as we have noted, a Board of Control—the foundation on which the India Office was eventually to arise. With power passing into the hands of the Government, it was manifestly at this point that the fortunes of the East India Company began to decline. Economic events hastened the process. With the coming of the Industrial Revolution India acquired significance as a market for British manufactured goods rather than as a supplier of spices, saltpetre, and silks. The trend was all in favour of industrial enterprise, competition and free trade; and the position of the Company, with its monopoly, was clearly anachronistic.

The great upheavals caused by the French Revolution also worked against the Company, by hampering trade and exposing its fleet of East Indiamen to enemy attack. Nevertheless, as the bicentenary of its foundation approached it was far from being a spent force. Indeed, some of its responsibilities went on increasing as one Indian State after another fell under British rule.

Arthur Wellesley, later to become Duke of Wellington, is an outstanding figure at the end of the century. He was not, of course, a servant of the Company, as Clive and Warren

Hastings had been, but a professional army officer, looking to Whitehall instead of Leadenhall Street for his orders. Wellesley arrived in India in 1796 with the rank of colonel, and, operating from Madras, moved against Mysore, which still constituted a threat. Sultan Hyder Ali had died in 1782, and was succeeded by his son Tippoo Sahib who, in league with the French, still dreamed of forcing the British out of India. Three English-commanded armies advanced, in the summer of 1799, on the capital, Seringapatam, and took it by assault. Wellesley, though only in charge of a small native force, emerged as the hero of the conquest of Mysore, for it was he who broke through the enemy defences. He was afterwards placed in command of an expedition against the Mahrattas, and in April 1803, took their capital, Poona. After fierce engagements at Assaye, Argaum and Gawilghur, resistance ended and peace with the Mahrattas was then concluded.

These victories had the effect of bringing enormous new areas and populations under the sway of the Company, which was obliged to increase its staff considerably. More English officers and more Sepoy soldiers were required to swell the ranks of the army in India; thousands of officials had to be recruited for assessing, imposing, and collecting taxes; and a whole regiment of others were needed to cope with the extension of the trading activities into the newly-acquired regions. In London, at East India House, there was a corresponding rise in the numbers of correspondents, controllers, accountants and clerks.

Yet, despite all the signs of augmented power and grandeur, the sands were running out fast. India had been won by the Company's men, but battles nearer home were, one by one, irretrievably lost. Lord Liverpool in 1813 passed a Bill through Parliament which gave the Board of Control authority over the Company's commercial activities and, to the great joy of the interlopers, abolished its monopoly of the India trade.

Finally, in 1833, the special trading privileges in regard to the China trade were terminated, and the East India Company was then left with only one major function—the administration of the Indian territories and the training of a 'civil service' for that purpose.

Rather surprisingly, it was not until the early part of the nineteenth century, when the East India Company was well past its heyday, that any great thought was given to the question of educating the administrators and executives upon whom it so considerably relied. It was, in fact, only when the Indian Empire had expanded to such an extent as to be almost unmanageable that appropriate action was taken. East India College was founded in 1805, in the village of Hailey, near Hertford, and the buildings, which still stand, provide ample evidence of the Company's power, opulence and dignity.

The sixty-acre site was a convenient one, only nineteen miles from the Leadenhall Street headquarters. On 12 May 1806 the foundation stone was laid by Charles Grant, who was a Member of Parliament and also an East India Company director. An architect steeped in the Greek tradition was made responsible for the construction of the building, which, like the colleges of Oxford and Cambridge, was designed so that its rooms and offices overlooked a quadrangle. When completed in 1809 a small group of students at once took up residence.

Great importance was attached to Haileybury as an educational and training centre. When, in 1813, the Company was again confirmed in its charter rights for a further term, specific mention of it was made in an act of Parliament passed to redefine the Company's legal status. Among other things, this Act provided that 'it should not be lawful for the Court of Directors to appoint to the Presidencies of Fort William, Fort St. George, or Bombay, any person in the capacity of a writer, unless such person should have been duly entered at such College, and have resided there four terms . . . and should produce at the expiration of that time a certificate under the hand of the Principal of the College, testifying that he had for the space of four terms been a member of the College, and conformed to the rules and regulations thereof.'

This enactment had subsequently to be suspended, because the vacancies for writers in the Presidencies far exceeded the number of young men qualified by the stipulated four terms' residence.

Among the more eminent professors who instructed the

students was Robert Malthus, famous for his *Essay on the Principles of Population*, in which he maintained that population increases in geometrical ratio, whereas food supply increases only in arithmetical ratio. This is an issue that has again leapt into prominence in recent years, because of the 'population explosion' in India and other Far Eastern countries.

The subjects taught at Haileybury included classical literature, mathematics, natural philosophy, political economy, English law and general history. Particular emphasis was laid on the study of Oriental languages, and students were required to learn the elements of Persian (in every case) and of Hindustani, Bengali, or Sanskrit, according to the Presidency to which they expected to be appointed. Arabic was also taught, and special prizes were awarded to those who acquired proficiency in its use.

Details of this kind make it clear that the East India Company, at that time, required its servants to be well educated. Many were, in fact, men of the highest capacity and integrity. Others failed lamentably, once they reached India, in applying their abilities: a few stupidly abused the trust reposed in them, and, by their errors and lack of imagination, precipitated events that were to terminate the Company's existence.

XVII

The charter was renewed for the last time in 1853, at a moment when the grand climax had already been prepared and was inevitable. India—notwithstanding the arrival there of the steamboats, railways, and electric telegraph—had been converted into a predominantly agricultural country. Its former prosperous cotton industry and extensive foreign trade had gone, and even the traditional handicrafts were in decline. British rule, direct or indirect, was everywhere established.

The strange dichotomy by which that rule was shared between the East India Company and the English Parliament persisted. Over the years, of course, the Government's influence had become greater, while that of the Company had diminished to the point where few, if any, of its traditional rights were left. Virtually, it had long ceased to be a trading enterprise, and acted as a quasi-Government agency, responsible for governing India and training a civil service.

Immense changes had taken place in India since Clive's victory at Plassey a hundred years earlier, and the life of the native masses had been profoundly disturbed. Seeing the old, established ways challenged and replaced by new, they became confused, restive; while the religious leaders, Brahmin and Moslem, openly expressed their disapproval. By the mid-nineteenth century intense social pressures had developed, and the more far-seeing Company officials, aware of this, did what they could to prevent an explosion. Others were deplorably tactless.

On 29th January 1857 the great revolt which we now refer to as the Indian Mutiny began. A British officer was murdered by the Sepoys under his command, and from that initial act of violence sprang a multitude of others. There were senseless massacres, executions, lootings, and destruction of property. The mutineers released criminals from the jails, set fire to the homes of British officials, and cut the telegraph lines. At Cawnpore, on the Ganges, where three regiments refused to obey orders, fierce fighting broke out. Sir Hugh Wheeler, the commander, withstood a siege of three weeks' duration, and then, accepting an offer to evacuate the garrison, was attacked. The entire force, combatant and non-combatant, was massacred—not even the women being spared. The brutal killings were matched, when Cawnpore was eventually relieved, by equally brutal reprisals.

Lucknow, forty-three miles north-east of Cawnpore, was another centre of revolt. In Delhi, where an aged Mogul Emperor, deprived of all authority, still nominally occupied the throne, there was an attempt to seize a large ammunition dump, but this was foiled by the resolute action of officials who destroyed it before making good their escape. In September, Delhi was recaptured, and any hopes that the Indians may have had of restoring the Mogul dynasty were finally shattered.

There remained only the hunting down of such rebel groups as continued to wage guerilla warfare, and the general pacification of the country. This took some time, but towards the end of 1858 the Mutiny, that last desperate attempt of Indians to regain their independence by force, was over. Ended, too, forever were the unique powers, responsibilities and privileges of the chartered adventurers.

XVIII

An 'Act for the better Government of India' had already been passed while the Mutiny was in progress. This provided for the supersession of the Directors and the Board of Control by a Secretary of State for India with a Council of fifteen experienced persons, the appointment of the Governor-General by the Crown, and the transference to the Crown of the Company's military and naval forces. On 1st November 1858 Queen Victoria was proclaimed as sovereign in all the main Indian cities. She assumed the title of Empress eighteen years later, and took the vast country, with its teeming millions, under her control.

The Company's last day of existence was 2nd August 1858, when the administrative functions it had exercised since 1833 were formally taken over by Crown officials. The 'Merchants of London trading into East India', the dividends on their capital secured on the Indian revenues, then made their exit from the imperial scene. East India House, in Leadenhall Street, which had been the nerve-centre, passed into the hands of the Secretary of State, to be later abandoned and pulled down to make way for a new building. Haileybury College, in Hertfordshire, where writers had been trained and taught Oriental languages, was converted into a public school.

Today, little remains of the great corporation, with its complex and romantic history, beyond a collection of old minute books, despatches, inventories and accounts in a Government archive.

* 7 *

Adventurers to Virginia

THE name that immediately leaps to mind in connection
with Virginia is, of course, that of Sir Walter Raleigh,
favourite courtier of Queen Elizabeth, navigator, merchant
adventurer, and historian. Twice he associated himself with
Sir Humphrey Gilbert, who was his half-brother, in expeditions
to the American continent. Though both ended in failure,
Raleigh persevered, and in 1584 sent a small fleet to explore the
Florida coast. This third expedition met with success. A
great area of land was formally annexed, to which, with
Elizabeth's consent, the name Virginia was given.

Raleigh, in the two or three years that followed this voyage,
made determined efforts to colonise Virginia, but was again
dogged by bad luck and, after losing £40,000, had to abandon
his plans, leaving their accomplishment to other and later
adventurers.

There were, however, two points of economic interest
arising out of Raleigh's voyages, not without their importance
for the future. One was the addition of the potato to the
Englishman's diet, and the second of tobacco to his addictions.

II

For a time, after these initial explorations, Virginia was forgotten. Already it was known that the country was not rich
in precious metals as had been hoped. Raleigh in 1602 sent
out another vessel. At the same time one was sailing under the
orders of a syndicate headed by the Earl of Southampton,
and this met with at least a measure of success, for friendly

relations with the Red Indians, with the prospect of profitable trade, were established.

This favourable outcome of the expedition acted as a spur to the merchants generally and, in 1606, applications for royal charters were made by two separate groups of adventurers desirous of trading with Virginia—one formed in London, and the other in the West Country. James I was pleased to grant the charters, which authorised both bodies to attempt settlements: the 'First Colony' to be the concern of London, and the 'Second Colony' to be the concern of Plymouth and the outports.

Those who wanted to become settlers had to go at their own expense, either in groups or as individuals, and the joint stock principle was not invoked until the exchange of commodities began. At first the trade was, of necessity, one-way only—goods being despatched to Virginia and little coming back. The cargoes were unloaded on arrival into a magazine or store, which also acted as a distributive centre. The treasurer, or 'cape merchant' as he was called, remitted the amounts collected from the colonists to the mother country.

With the London company, which founded Jamestown on 14th May, 1607, things did not go too well at first—for the obstacles to be overcome were much greater than had been foreseen. Apart from Red Indian hostility, difficulties were experienced with the emigrants—a motley crowd, far more interested in the discovery of gold or silver than in the laborious pursuit of agriculture. No wonder, then, that the hopes of the adventurers for quick returns on their money were dashed and that, for a time, they made nothing but losses. Fortunately, the governor of the colony, Captain John Smith, was a man of character, and ruled the little community with firmness and ability. He had been captured, soon after the landing in Virginia, by Red Indian braves, and but for the intervention of the chief's daughter, Pocahontas, would almost certainly have been killed.

Despite the bad start, the adventurers were determined to go on, and in 1609 they obtained a second charter authorising them to form a joint stock company under the title: 'The Treasurer and Company of Planters of the City of London for the First Colony in Virginia'. They were empowered to arrange for the transportation of settlers from England, to survey and distribute the land, and to trade. The first Council and treasurer were nominated by the Crown, but afterwards directors and officers could be elected at the Company's own discretion.

While this second charter was being negotiated, steps were taken to infuse new enthusiasm into the Virginia colonization scheme, and to attract fresh finance. The early subscribers were promised large allocations of land and, as an added inducement, that their names would be written into the charter. Tradesmen who adventured their persons, as distinct from their capital, were to receive one hundred acres of land. Even more generous grants were offered to 'persons of quality' who might be tempted to start life afresh in the new colony. Shares in the Company were £12. 10. 0 each.

Much interest was displayed in the *Nova Britannia* to be established on the other side of the ocean. Finance was quickly forthcoming, and in May, 1609, Sir Thomas Gates set sail from London with a fleet of eight ships. On board were six hundred men, and we can imagine the high hopes that followed the expedition. Once again, however, the results were disappointing, and part of the fleet returned 'laden with nothing but bad reports'. The adventurers, discouraged and gloomy, were disinclined for further voyages.

When the time came to make further calls on the capital each had agreed to subscribe, there were many defaulters. Some with excessive optimism, had hoped to pay the second instalments out of the first profits. Difficulties arose, and the Governor of the Company was obliged to borrow money so that another expedition, led by Lord de la Warr, could be equipped. This was in 1610. A year later it became obvious that, if the rich and fertile lands of Virginia were to be exploited to the full, capital funds far in excess of any estimate yet made would have to be raised. A sum as high as £30,000 was mentioned, to be raised over a period of two years.

III

A critical point had been reached, but at least one item of good news arrived to lighten the mood of depression. One of the eight ships that had sailed in 1609, under Sir Thomas Gates, had been wrecked in the Bermudas, or Somers Islands as they were then called, some six hundred miles off the American coast. Sir George Somers, commander of the wrecked vessel— and, indeed, the emigrants generally—found the position a congenial one and decided to stay. Somers despatched a report to London, in which he praised the fertility of the soil and the excellent fishing to be had. Moreover, it soon became apparent that the Bermudas, adequately fortified, were well placed strategically for the defence of Virginia, should the Spaniards develop their threatened attack.

To build fortifications and install a garrison called for yet more capital. After careful deliberation, it was decided to form a subsidiary company, which, under the title 'Undertakers for the Plantation of the Somers Islands' was able to raise enough capital to send a ship and sixty men to establish a separate colony.

First, however, a legal obstacle had to be considered. The Virginia Company's charter only extended to a distance of one hundred miles from the mainland—and the islands, though they had been discovered by the Virginia Company, could not be claimed on its behalf. The adventurers had, therefore, to sell out their interests to the subsidiary—the Somers Islands Company—which, from the very first, began to prosper. It avoided some of the more glaring mistakes made by the parent company—no time, for instance, was wasted in the vain search for gold—and so, within a year of the shipwreck, a handsome profit could be recorded.

To some extent this was made possible by an accidental discovery. An enormous block of ambergris, weighing about 175 pounds and of the 'size and shape of a giant', was unearthed. Valued alike for its perfume and medicinal properties, ambergris was a semi-precious commodity, worth from £3 to £4 an ounce. The eventual proceeds provided a most welcome windfall, and there was further cause for congratulation when pearls were discovered in oyster beds adjoining the islands. Thus, while the affairs of the parent company were going from bad to worse, those of the subsidiary were in a quite flourishing condition.

Forts were constructed and work on the plantations began. The adventurers were prompt in paying their calls and, in 1614, to place themselves on firmer legal foundations, they petitioned for a separate charter. The Crown responded favourably, and on 29th September, they were incorporated as 'The Governor and Company of the City of London for the Plantation of the Somers Islands,' with Sir Thomas Smythe, treasurer of the Virginia Company, as first governor.

IV

Meantime, the parent company had been wrestling with the seemingly intractable problem of raising £30,000 for the development of its own mainland territories. A sum of £2,000 had been received from the Somers Islands Company, as consideration for the transfer of rights, but this was a mere drop in the ocean of Virginia's needs. Moreover, hardly had the money changed hands than the legality of the transaction was queried, because of the 100-mile limit, beyond which the Virginia Company was not authorised to act.

To rectify this particular matter, and also to obtain powers to raise money by means of lotteries, the directors applied for a third charter. Granted in 1612, it sanctioned the lotteries and, further, provided that all exports from England to Virginia were, for a space of seven years, to be exempt from Customs duties, a concession which it was hoped would encourage the adventurers.

Action was then taken to raise the money so urgently required. In June, 1612, the first of the lotteries was organised, with only moderate success. Yet, the adventurers being completely apathetic, the Company was obliged for some time to continue with the lotteries, in order that the colony might be kept supplied. However, a turning point in the fortunes of Virginia was reached quite unexpectedly.

The planters had raised an experimental crop of tobacco, and in 1613 sent the first consignment home, quite unaware that it was to be their salvation. London liked the Virginian tobacco and was willing to pay for it at the rate of three shillings a pound.

Interest in the Virginia Company immediately revived, and adventurers, both with and without capital, began to cross the Atlantic in force. They were, as already indicated, men of all sorts and conditions, ranging from the religious dissenter to the unruly gallant, sent abroad by his relatives to save him from the hangman's noose. The promised land-divisions were made and tobacco soon became a staple crop, to be exchanged through the 'magazine' and the cape merchant for goods from the mother country.

There were still vicissitudes ahead for the colonists, but with their settling down to agriculture, their future was assured. Among other things, they set up administrative machinery that was to endure right down to the time of the American revolution. In 1619, it may be added, negro slave-labour was introduced, and we see the beginnings of a social pattern that was to establish itself so firmly in later years, with the planter gradually assuming the status of an aristocrat.

V

A little later, in 1620, a quarrel appears to have broken out between the Virginia Company and the Somers Islands Company, but the details are complicated and largely concerned with the refusal of individualistic directors to agree on matters of policy. Of more general interest is the formation, in 1621, of a whole constellation of satellite companies to render aid to the Virginia Company which, because of the withdrawal of the right to hold lotteries, was again in financial straits. New capital was required, and these subsidiaries, each organised for a particular purpose, were to be the means of raising money from among the London adventurers. There was, for example, the 'Joint Stock for providing Apparel and other Necessaries', floated with a capital of £1,800, and expected to make good profits. Other companies had as their objective the manufacture of glass beads in Virginia, the sending of shipwrights to the colony, and the development of the fur trade.

One of the more unusual and enterprising subsidiaries was formed to ameliorate the hard lot of the colonists, predominantly male in composition, by ending their isolation from the fair sex.

This most worthy and humane venture was organised under the title 'The Joint Stock for transporting 100 Maids to be made Wives' and proved, as it deserved to be, a huge success. Prospective brides were sent to Virginia by the Company at a cost of approximately £12, which covered the passage and all incidental expenses. When suitable matches for the young women had been arranged each prospective husband handed over 150 pounds of tobacco, to recompense the adventurers for their trouble. Since the tobacco could be sold in London at 3s. a pound, it provided an ample margin of profit, and so everyone was satisfied. The Somers Islands Company promoted a similar undertaking.

VI

It will be remembered that King James's charter of 1606 had simultaneously conferred rights on two separate groups of adventurers, those of London, and those of the West Country. The Londoners had been granted lands in the southern part of Virginia, the West of England men territory in the north. While the fortunes of the former group have already been traced in some detail, it remains for at least something to be said about the Plymouth adventurers.

They had confined their early activities to trading and made no efforts to found a colony, one of the main reasons for this lack of initiative being that the adventurers were scattered about in towns over a wide area, and lacked cohesion. This imposed difficulties in the matter of raising finance. Leader of the second Virginia Company was Sir John Popham, who sent out a few ships, the commanders of which had instructions to search for mineral deposits and the north-west passage. One of Sir John's expeditionary fleets fell into the hands of the Spaniards, a second returned home with nothing accomplished, but a third, which sailed in May, 1607, made at least a landing and a temporary stay on the American coast. Between 1615 and 1620 the fisheries were profitably exploited, but no colony, comparable with that in the south, was established.

Eventually a new company was formed, the forty members of which were nominated by the Crown as 'persons of honour or gentlemen of blood.' They stepped, as it were, into the shoes of the second Virginia Company and assumed the title of 'The Council established at Plymouth, in the County of Devon, for the Planting, Ruling, Ordering, and Governing of New England.' The renaming of the territory (which corresponds roughly to the modern States of Maine, New Hampshire, Vermont, Massachusetts, Rhode Island and Connecticut) was made at the suggestion of Captain John Smith, who had carried out explorations in 1614. Immediately after incorporation, the Company endeavoured to raise capital in the West Country towns—but met with only a lukewarm response. This was due, in large measure, to the unpopularity of the nominated Council among the merchants and their friends. Not until 1623, after many delays, was a single fishing vessel equipped, and so the colonisation of New England seemed as far off as ever. It was left to a body of men since named 'the Pilgrim Fathers' to seize the initiative and succeed where others had failed.

VII

We must, for a moment, go back to the year 1620, when an approach was made to the Virginia Company for permission to settle in the northern territory. This permission had been granted to the applicants, a group of Puritans and non-conformists, who sought religious freedom and had in them, moreover, the true spirit of pioneers. These men formed themselves into a joint stock company, some brief account of which must now be given.

There was no formal incorporation by charter, but the way in which the joint stock was to regulate its affairs was defined in an agreement to which all subscribed. Three different types of members were enrolled—those who contributed money only, those who adventured their persons and could find £10 for their passage, and those who adventured their persons only. The shares were £10 each, and every adult in the expedition was regarded as the owner of at least one share. All profits made, and lands acquired, over a period of seven years, were to belong to the joint stock. Provision was made in the agreement for an equal division among the adventurers.

The emigrants, about one hundred in number, set sail in *The Mayflower* on 16th September 1620. Two months later they had safely crossed the Atlantic and were off the American coast. On 21st December they landed at Plymouth, Massachusetts, and colonisation of the northern half of Virginia was begun, quite independently, it will be observed, of the 'New England Company' and its 'persons of honour', from whom, however, a formal sanction had in due course to be obtained.

The pilgrims quickly established themselves, and their industry on the plantations ensured excellent progress. At the expiration of the seven years named in the agreement, the joint stock was wound up and the adventurers who had remained in England surrendered their rights in the colony.

Massachusetts, one of the original thirteen States of the Union, now covers an area of over 8,000 square miles, and is inhabited by eight million people. Many of them—particularly in Boston, the capital—are direct descendants of the early settlers who, like their counterparts in Virginia, gradually acquired aristocratic status. Even today these men, who were responsible for writing an inspiring chapter into both British and American history, continue to make their influence felt. The Puritan spirit—stern, uncompromising, independent—still lingers on in New England, like a flame that the great winds blowing down the centuries have been unable to put out.

* 8 *

Adventurers into Hudson's Bay

BY the time that James I succeeded Elizabeth to the English throne in 1603 explorers had sailed to some of the most distant parts of the world, and were beginning to understand the relationships between the great land masses and the oceans. Only two regions remained completely shrouded in mystery— i.e. the two formidable ice-bound wastes at the north and south poles. Antarctica, of course, was too far away—indeed, almost as remote as the other side of the moon—to excite European curiosity, but the far north had certainly done so throughout the sixteenth century. Men believed that Cathay and the South Seas could be reached by way of a north-east passage and also by way of a north-west passage.

Among the first men to seek out those fabled waterways was Henry Hudson, who ranks with Sir Martin Frobisher, William Baffin, and John Davis as one of the most intrepid of the early English explorers. The Muscovy Company, whose career has already been outlined, sent him in 1607 to discover, if he could, a way of reaching China along the north Asian coastline. Though that attempt was unsuccessful, he was commissioned by the Dutch East India Company in 1609 to sail westwards across the Atlantic in search of new territories. In September he reached New York Bay and sailed 150 miles up the river to which his name was later given. It was in 1610 that he left London in the *Discovery* and, having rounded the northernmost cape of Labrador, entered the great 'U' shaped Bight, which is such a prominent feature of the North American continent. When winter set in the ship became icebound, and the hardships then endured—including the intense cold, lack of food, and scurvy—culminated in a mutiny in the following spring. Hudson was cast adrift in the inhospitable Bay in an open boat and never heard of again. Half a century was to elapse, after that inauspicious beginning, before Hudson Bay was opened up as one of the world's richest fur-trading centres.

The stimulus came, strangely enough, from two obscure but resourceful French-Canadians, who had penetrated overland to the area between Hudson Bay and the Great Lakes in which the beaver, and other fur-bearing animals, were found in almost inexhaustible abundance. The two men—Médard Chouart des Groseilliers ('Mr Gooseberry' as he was later named in England) and Pierre Esprit Radisson—were tough, rough, and not perhaps too scrupulous where national loyalties were concerned, but it was through them, and their wanderings among the Indians in the forests and by the rivers of Canada, that the Hudson's Bay Company came into being.

II

To do them justice on the score of patriotism, Groseilliers and Radisson, who were brothers-in-law, had on returning to French Quebec reported their discoveries to the French Governor, who had been so much impressed by their story— and the proceeds of two years' trading piled up in their canoes—that he had hailed them as heroes. Guns had been fired in their honour; they had been feasted, flattered and entertained. Hardly, however, were the celebrations over than differences arose between the two pioneers and the Governor on the question of how the proceeds of future expeditions into the interior were to be divided.

Returning to Quebec after a second exploration, which took them into the great northern forest, with three hundred Indians and furs currently valued at £60,000, they were arrested and charged with the offence of trading without a licence. On this and other grounds they were heavily fined and deprived of the greater part of their hard-won spoils. It was this confiscation, manifestly high-handed and unjust, that decided the two French-Canadians to turn to England, with a view to interesting King Charles II in their plans for developing the Hudson Bay territory—a veritable Eldorado, as they believed—and establishing a series of trading depots there. First, however, Groseilliers crossed to France in an attempt to obtain redress from the French Government, and only when all his efforts had proved in vain did he and Radisson make their historic decision to seek other aid.

They arrived in London in 1666, the year of the Great Fire, were presented to Sir George Carteret and by him to the king. They told their story, were given a sympathetic hearing, and then entered into somewhat long-drawn-out and inconclusive discussions. At last, in 1667, the matter was taken up by Prince Rupert, the king's brilliant cousin. Sensing the territorial as well as the trading possibilities in North America, he urged Charles and the gentlemen of the Court, to act on the information Groseilliers and Radisson had provided and form themselves into a syndicate.

A ship of the Royal Navy, the *Eaglet*, was then placed at their disposal and accompanied by another vessel named the *Nonsuch* she sailed from Gravesend in June 1668 with instructions to assess the prospects of opening up a profitable fur trade, but also to discover, if possible 'the north-west Passage to the South Seas' which, despite the failure of earlier explorers, the learned men of the Royal Society, poring over their primitive maps and charts, were confident existed.

Almost at the end of the voyage, when they were in Hudson Strait, the two ships ran into a storm, and the *Eaglet* sustained such heavy damage that she was obliged to turn back. However, the *Nonsuch*, a ketch of only fifty tons, was able to continue the voyage. She reached James Bay where her captain, Zachariah Gillam of Boston, and his crew spent the winter, while Groseilliers (Radisson was on the *Eaglet*) made contact with the natives. In exchange for various English commodities —weapons, tools and trinkets—he received a supply of beaver skins which, at that time, were in fashionable demand for the manufacture of felt hats. No sooner had the ice broken in the Rupert River, in the spring of 1669, than the *Nonsuch* departed for home, with every stitch of canvas set. Though loaded to the waterline, she crossed the Atlantic without incident and was back at an English port on 9th October—without having discovered the North West Passage but with convincing proof that in Hudson Bay, and the territory surrounding it, there existed commercial possibilities of a quite exeptional order.

Looking over the cargo, the courtier-adventurers were well satisfied with the success of the expedition. The outcome was that, on 2nd May, 1670, the king granted them a charter by which they were incorporated as *The Governor and Company of Adventurers of England trading into Hudson's Bay*. This document—covering five parchment sheets and still carefully preserved—conferred on Prince Rupert and his seventeen associates the 'sole trade and commerce of Hudson's Bay', with all the adjacent lands, territories and countries, discovered or undiscovered, including the mineral rights and the fisheries. These powers, as in the case of the East India Company, were on a truly imperial scale.

Rupert himself was appointed as first Governor of the new company, which was organized on a joint stock basis. The Duke of Albemarle, the Earl of Craven, Lord Arlington and Lord Ashley were among the 'true and absolute lords and proprietors'. The name of plain John Portman, Citizen and Goldsmith of London, appears at the foot of a long and aristocratic list as the corporations' first treasurer.

III

The original capital of the Hudson's Bay Company was £10,500, and this was at once used to equip further expeditions. However, the development of the Company proceeded along slow and cautious lines—which is rather surprising when we remember that its Governor had an established reputation as a dashing and impetuous cavalry leader. Very small fleets, or sometimes only single vessels, left Gravesend every spring, and arrived at their destination in the autumn, just prior to the first snowfalls and the formation of the ice. The captains were placed in charge of cargoes made up of such things as knives, kettles, hatchets, fowling pieces, flints—and, at a later stage, beads, blankets, tobacco, and brandy, this last-named commodity with most unhappy consequences. The vessels wintered in Hudson Bay, and returned to England with cargoes of assorted furs. Though beaver was the most important, musquash, mink, fox, ermine (formerly restricted to royalty, and still a part of almost all state robes), wolverine, otter and lynx pelts were included. After reaching London, which quickly developed into the fur market for Central Europe, the furs were graded and sold—at first privately but later at public auctions.

Garraway's Coffee House, in the City, was one of the earliest venues for these auctions. There, in December 1671, Prince Rupert, the Duke of York, and other gentlemen of the Court, assembled for the first time to watch while 'thirty Lotts of Beaver Skins' were 'knocked down' to the highest bidder—though, to be accurate, the sales were not, as we say today 'under the hammer' but 'by the candle'. The poet Dryden was present at this famous Coffee House auction, and commemorated it in a few lines of verse.

For the first fourteen years of its existence, the Hudson's Bay Company was able to trade in comparatively calm and settled conditions. Trading posts were set up at various points on the coasts of the Bay—Fort Nelson (later to be renamed York Factory), Moose Factory, Rupert's House, Albany Factory—and, at a later stage, many more in the as yet unexplored interior. At home, the directors were able to make handsome dividend distributions, especially towards the end of the century. On one occasion, for example, they declared a 'two for one' bonus issue of stock, and paid a dividend of 25 per cent on this tripled capital, making a true dividend of 75 per cent. These incredibly high earnings caused the stockholders to be regarded with not a little envy.

Already, too, dark mutterings were being heard in the City of London over the Company's monopoly, its wide-ranging powers, immense territorial holdings, and exclusiveness. On the other side of the Atlantic more serious troubles were brewing, for the French-Canadians, who had a colony on the St. Lawrence River, were beginning to make their hostility felt. Competition between the French and English traders, indeed, became so fierce that it led to violence.

On several occasions the French launched full-scale and

well organized attacks, with a view to dislodging the Hudson Bay men from their positions. The settlements were raided, the vessels from England waylaid and sunk. In 1689 the adventurers complained to King William III that 'according to their true and exact estimate' the French had taken from them in the six previous years no less than 'seven ships with their cargoes, and six forts and factories from which they carried away great stores of goods'. What made the attacks and depredations particularly galling was the fact that they occurred at a time when England and France were 'at full peace'.

An unusually determined effort to expel the English traders from their bases in Hudson Bay and Prince Rupert's Land was made by the French Colonial Governor Frontenac in 1697. Five men-of-war entered the Bay and struck at a squadron of four English vessels which had only just made the Atlantic crossing. The engagement ended in disaster for the Company, two of its ships and all the forts except one falling into enemy hands. By that time, of course, the two home countries were at war, and this episode may therefore be regarded as merely an extension of the larger conflict.

For many years prior to 1718 the Company made little profit and was unable to pay dividends. However, the European victories of the Duke of Marlborough—who was Governor of the Hudson's Bay Company from 1685 to 1692—and the Treaty of Utrecht, signed in 1713, were turning points, for a clause in the Treaty provided that Hudson Bay should remain English territory.

In the thirty years of peace that followed, the Company had the opportunity of restoring its broken fortunes. By the time that war broke out again in 1744 the various forts had been strengthened and the defenders, having been well trained in the use of cannon and small arms, were prepared for all contingencies.

IV

Meanwhile, at home, rival interests were sharply criticising the Company's monopoly and voicing demands for an enquiry to be made into its affairs. The chorus of abuse rose to a crescendo in the 1740s, one of the more persistent attackers being Arthur Dobbs, a wealthy Irishman who, as it later transpired, himself aspired to form a company with exclusive trading privileges. A man of enquiring mind, he appears to have had an intense interest in discovering a way to China and the South Seas by way of the North West Passage, in the existence of which he had an almost fanatical belief.

As far back as 1737, Dobbs had been the means of prodding the Hudson's Bay Company into action in regard to this important charter obligation. He had forced the directors, against their better judgment, to equip two sloops, the *Churchill* and the *Musquash*, in an endeavour to chart a course through the islands and icefloes. They returned without having discovered anything of importance, and the Company, convinced that there was no North West Passage, let the matter drop—an attitude that only served to stimulate Arthur Dobbs to yet further denunciation.

Finally, Parliament offered a reward of £20,000 for the discovery of the North West Passage, whereupon Dobbs formed a company and equipped two vessels, the *Dobbs* and the *California*, in a bid to succeed where the Hudson's Bay Company had so conspicuously failed. The expedition returned to England in 1747, baffled and defeated, yet still expressing—in ambiguous terms—its conviction that a passage to the Pacific, across the roof of the North American continent, did in fact exist.

On 10th March 1749, the Company's minute book recorded that a motion had been carried in the House of Commons, for an enquiry into 'the state and condition of the countries and trade of Hudson Bay, and into the rights the Company pretend to have by charter to the property of land and exclusive trade', and further, that the committee of enquiry was actually appointed.

The fight was now on in real earnest, and the Hudson's Bay Company, which had at first tried to confound its critics by maintaining a majestic silence, was called upon to divulge its affairs and state its case.

Briefly, the charges were that the Company had made insufficient effort to discover the North West Passage; had not extended the settlements to the extent contemplated by the charter; had by the latter failure encouraged French infiltration into the Hudson Bay area; had not pushed the trade with sufficient vigour; and, finally, had demoralised the Red Indians and ill-treated its own servants. This formidable indictment placed a heavy work-load on the shoulders of the Committee, which, not unnaturally, took such short cuts as it could.

The last two accusations were virtually ignored. Humanitarianism was not yet the force it was to become later in the eighteenth century, when enlightened men attacked the slave trade and sought to ameliorate the excessive punishments inflicted for minor offences. The fact that employees might be beaten for acts of indiscipline, or that the Red Indians were being debauched by 'fire water', meant little or nothing. The other complaints, however, received close attention.

The conclusions of the Parliamentary Committee were disappointing for Dobbs and his allies. With an eye on the manoeuvres of the French in North America, the Government had decided that the Company must, at all costs, be supported. Accordingly, no serious negligence or corruption having been brought to light, the Hudson's Bay Company was confirmed in all its rights. The crisis was overcome, and Dobbs—whose trenchant criticism had been aimed at achieving free trade— was obliged to keep the peace forever after. When he was appointed Governor of North Carolina, his undoubted abilities were diverted into more constructive channels.

v

During the 1750s the Hudson's Bay Company began to probe into the remote interior of its allotted territories. At first, these were no more than one-man expeditions, which often failed, but occasionally yielded really worth-while results. One of the first such exploratory trips into the forests and prairies lying westwards was made by Anthony Henday, an English ex-smuggler, who left York Factory in June, 1754, at the head of a group of Indians in an attempt to capture a larger proportion of the fur trade from the French traders, who were very enterprising. Henday, travelling by canoe up the Hayes River, reached

Saskatchewan and Alberta, came within sight of the Rocky
Mountains, and after wintering in the far west was back at
Hudson Bay just a year later. Though he achieved little in the
commercial sense, his journey added something to the limited
store of knowledge then available about North America, for he
kept a detailed journal. In this he described, among other
things, how the Red Indians hunted buffalo on horseback. His
colleagues found it hard to believe this, though they were full
of admiration for the courage and initiative he had displayed.

Another Company man, William Pink, left York factory in
1766 on a similar mission, i.e. in search of trade, and, journey-
ing on foot, reached the Athabasca River country. Samuel
Hearne's journey to the Coppermine River in search of
rumoured copper deposits in regions close to the arctic circle
was another bold and adventurous undertaking. Having staked
a claim, on behalf of the Company, to the lands he had discovered, he returned safely to Prince of Wales's Fort some
eighteen months later. Eventually, he was placed in command
of Prince of Wales's Fort—a massive stone stronghold with
walls between thirty and forty feet thick, which still stands.
It is now owned and maintained by the Dominion of Canada as
a monument of historical interest. Hearne, it may be added,
was also the founder of Cumberland House, on the Saskatchewan river, the Company's first interior trading post.

Altogether, in the years 1754–1774, the Hudson's Bay
Company sponsored sixty inland expeditions with a view to
stimulating the Indian trade. In subsequent decades further
explorations resulted in the establishment of forts at more
than one hundred different places—ranging from the Atlantic
to the Pacific coasts, from the U.S. boundary to the arctic
circle.

VI

Though the commercial prospects improved considerably after
Wolfe's capture of Quebec and defeat of the French-Canadians,
the Company ran into fresh difficulties when other traders, of
English and Scottish origin, settled in the North West of the
country and began competitive trading. In course of time these
independent groups were drawn together by their many

common interests. In 1784 they formed the North West Company based in Montreal, and challenged the Hudson's Bay Company on its own terrain. Rough, tough and daring, these traders quickly built up a powerful and successful organization which covered the entire country. With characteristic arrogance they build their forts alongside those of the English chartered adventurers—who were regarded as foreigners. Failing to achieve their purpose by argument, they staged a series of provocations—court actions, seizures of land and property, and assaults on personnel.

The Hudson's Bay Company met these attacks, in the first instance, with admirable restraint, but eventually had to retaliate in kind. Blow was returned for blow and plot met with counterplot. At last, the rivalry became so bitter that it was culminated in armed conflict. The massacre of peaceful settlers, who had made their homes on the Red River, by North West Company men—mostly half-breeds—was one of the more alarming of such incidents.

A young Scotsman of philanthropic disposition—Thomas Douglas, fifth Earl of Selkirk—had been moved by the plight of the Scottish crofters, evicted from their homes at the time of the Highland clearances. After a first and successful attempt on Prince Edward's Island, he worked out a plan for settling emigrants from Scotland in the Canadian territories.

He began by purchasing stock of the Hudson's Bay Company in amounts large enough to give him a controlling interest. In May 1811 the directors granted him, in fee simple, over one-hundred-thousand square miles for the establishment of the proposed colony. The site chosen for building the first log huts was at the junction of the Red and Assiniboine rivers, at the very spot on which Winnipeg, the capital of Manitoba, was later to arise.

VII

The North West traders included in their ranks men of the highest calibre. One of the most determined and dynamic was Alexander Mackenzie who, in 1789, left Fort Chipewyan on Lake Athabaska and, descending by the river that now bears his name, reached the arctic. Four years later, he made

history by working his way across the Rockies and reaching
Dean Channel on the Pacific coast. There, to make sure that his
achievement would not be overlooked by posterity, he carved
his name and the date—22nd July, 1793—on a rock. Subsequently, when he visited London, he was hailed as one of the
foremost traders of his time and honoured with a knighthood.

Mackenzie, when he heard of the proposed Red River
colony, which the Hudson's Bay Company supported, reacted
very sharply. He protested that the settlement would block the
lines of communication between Montreal, where he and his
associates had their headquarters, and the North West, from
which they obtained their furs. Though Selkirk was despised
as an impractical idealist, a sentimentalist, and a radical,
the North West men yet chose to see in him a dangerous enemy,
who threatened not only their trade but their very existence.

Despite Selkirk's expressly stated lack of interest in the
fur trade, which in fact he abhorred, the North West Company
was determined to break both him and the attempt at colonization. The first party of emigrants left Stornoway in 1811;
a second sailed in 1812, and a third in 1814—the total number
of people involved being only about one hundred. Shortly
after their arrival in Canada, the Governor of the Selkirk
Colony issued a decree prohibiting the export of pemmican,
the dried buffalo-beef on which the traders both of the North
West and Hudson Bay, largely subsisted, and relations were
immediately strained to breaking point. The North West
men then embarked on a course of action which aimed at
nothing less than the physical extermination of the Red River
colonists.

In June, 1817, a raiding party, encouraged by the North
West Company, swooped down on the settlers and killed about
thirty of them—including the local Governor, Robert Semple—
in circumstances of great brutality. This treacherous attack
—the 'Massacre of Seven Oaks'—took place quite near to what
is now the main street of Winnipeg, and caused great indignation. Those responsible were, however, never brought to justice,
and the vendetta was terminated only when the two rival
trading organizations decided to bury the hatchet and unite.

Selkirk's noble dream of a free agricultural community,
c.c.—8

based on democratic principles, was shattered, and in due course the Hudson's Bay Company bought back the land. He himself, after the massacre, was dragged through the Montreal law courts on one pretext and another. At last, he was obliged to return home, unable to carry on the unequal struggle because of ruined health, though undefeated in spirit. Not until after his death in 1820 did the settlement of Assiniboia which he had founded strike firm roots and begin to flourish.

VIII

The amalgamation of the North West Company and the Hudson's Bay Company took place in 1821, and the wasteful competition which had hampered the development of both then ceased. Parliament in that year granted the united Company a licence to trade for twenty-one years in the regions to the west and north of its existing territories. As a result, monopoly rights were acquired over half a continent, and the fur traders then entered into one of their greatest and most prosperous periods. Their 'empire' included the whole of modern Canada, excepting only the basin of the Great Lakes and the maritime provinces. Though primarily traders, they were also administrators of the area.

Supreme control of the Hudson's Bay Company remained, of course, with the Governor, Deputy Governor and Committee in London, as before. The old name, the royal charter, and the flag were retained, but there had inevitably to be a considerable amount of internal reorganization. Much of this work was undertaken by George (later Sir George) Simpson, a Scotsman, who had gone to Canada in 1820 and was appointed, shortly after the merger, to a position of responsibility. Eventually, he became Governor in Chief and, until 1860, continued to play a dominant role in the Company's affairs.

One of his first acts was to withdraw the garrisons of half-breeds from the forts, and put them to work on the land. He also closed down the superfluous trading posts; retired many of the Company's older employees on pension, and inaugurated a stricter system of financial control. Sir George—he was knighted by Queen Victoria in 1841—also travelled extensively, and encouraged exploration in all the more remote and inaccessible parts of Canada—in and beyond the Rockies, in British Columbia, along the Alaskan border, and—with a view to determining the northern coastline—in the arctic.

Under Simpson's wise and forceful administration Canada began to develop, and the Hudson's Bay Company rose to what was probably the peak point of its career. The time arrived, however, when its highly privileged position—and the monopoly, with its restrictive effects—were again challenged. By the middle of the nineteenth century, when thousands of emigrants were settling in Canada and towns were springing up all over the prairies, Government rule by a group of fur traders was clearly seen to be anachronistic. In 1857, after charges of maladministration had been laid before the British Government, a Select Committee of the House of Commons was appointed to investigate the affairs of the Hudson's Bay Company. Prominent men such as W. E. Gladstone and Lord John Russell sat on this Committee, which spent five months in considering the complex problems involved.

The outcome, briefly, was that Vancouver Island, where a colony had been founded under the Company's aegis in 1849, was repossessed by the Crown; the licence covering the monopoly of the North West territories was allowed to lapse, and the Company was restricted to the trade and administration of Rupert's Land—even those diminished rights being hedged about with reservations.

Parliament, having listened to Sir George Simpson—who was principal witness at the 'trial'—considered that the interests of the settlers, and not those of the fur traders, would have to be paramount, and so the Company's position, in the political sense, was a little eroded. Obviously, the monopoly it had enjoyed since 1670 could not much longer resist the advancing tide of progress.

IX

Ten years passed without any further significant change in the Company's legal status. The population of the territory, however, continued to increase at a fairly rapid rate, swelled by successive waves of migration, not only from Britain but from the U.S.A., until by 1869—two years after Confederation under the British-North America Act—there were approximately 1½ million people living in the English-speaking part of Canada, and one million in the French-speaking part. Most of the major cities—Montreal, Winnipeg, Vancouver—were firmly established and Ottawa was functioning as the capital. Fur trading, though still important, was being largely supplanted by agriculture and industry. Soon Canada, young and thrusting, was again chafing at the fetters that still bound her to a group of London stockholders.

The inevitable revision of the Company's monopoly came in 1869, when certain rights, though not the charter itself, were relinquished. Under the Deed of Surrender, which received the royal assent in 1870, the territories reverted to the Crown, and were then transferred to the Canadian Government, which compensated the Company by making a grant of £300,000 and one-twentieth part of the land in any township settled within the fertile belt. The Company was left in control of the trading posts, and allowed to carry on as a private trading corporation without hindrance or exceptional taxation of its land, trade or servants. Relieved of all administrative responsibilities, it was able to concentrate on purely commercial activities. In many ways, as it turned out, the changes tended to enlarge, rather than reduce, the Company's opportunities and the scale of its operations.

X

During the thirty years that followed the Deed of Surrender, Canada moved forward, with the rest of the world, into the new era of steam and electricity. Railways—notably the Canadian-Pacific, completed in 1885—and telegraphs were laid across the 3,000 miles separating the west and east coasts, with revolutionary effects on speed of communication and transport. Vast changes began to take place, and the Hudson's Bay Company, exposed from that point onwards to every form of competition, had either to meet the challenge or pass out of existence. The fur trade, of course, continued as a leading activity, but the directors decided, very wisely, to branch out in other directions and diversify the Company's interests. A very natural departure, in view of the populous communities developing round the old trading forts, was the Company's entry into the chain store business.

One of the first and most typical stores was that at Edmonton —opened early in the 1890s, just after the Canadian-Pacific Railway had arrived. Originally housed in an unpretentious building in Jasper Avenue, it had to be enlarged a few years later when the Klondike gold-rush began. Hundreds of prospectors then besieged the store for equipment and provisions needed on the long and hazardous journey to the goldfields. Edmonton grew so fast that again, in 1904, a new and larger store had to be built. The merchandise was of a general nature, with still a certain emphasis on such things as rum, plaid shawls, blankets, coloured feathers and beads for the redskins. There were large glass mirrors, elevators and other civilized refinements in this Edmonton store, which, as the years went by, had to be continually expanded.

The nucleus of the Winnipeg store, now the most important, was completed in 1881, and greatly enlarged at the turn of the century. Though much of the floor space was at first used for storage purposes, the front of the building was for retail business. In 1911, new and more ample accommodation in Main Street had to be provided. Fifteen years later the Hudson's Bay Company built an entirely new store in Winnipeg, designed to serve a population of 250,000 people, which turned out to be one of the best and most modern retail stores in the country. At Hudson's Bay House, not far from Garry Gate in Winnipeg, is the Company's Canadian head office.

Today the Hudson's Bay Company's wholesale, retail and multiple store activities greatly exceed the fur trade, important though that still is. All kinds of consumer goods are stocked: clothing, hardware, drugs, foodstuffs, jewellery, flowers, pianos and books. Customers have the use of restaurants, cafeterias, and multi-storey car-parks, which give direct access to the stores.

Though, eventually, the Hudson's Bay Company sold most of the seven million acres of land acquired after the Deed of

Surrender, it retained the mineral rights, and these may well prove, in the near future, to be extremely valuable. Prospecting in recent years has revealed the existence of oil in considerable quantities and many wells are already in full production.

XI

The date on which it had been agreed that transfer of the Company's land and authority should become effective was 1st December 1869, but the arrangements had left out of account a minority group; the Red River half-breeds who, uneasy as to their future under Canadian rule, rose up in armed rebellion. Led by Louis Riel, they captured Fort Garry and set up a 'provisional Government' which tried to assert its authority over the whole country. They saw their traditional free way of life—essentially that of hunters— threatened by the influx of thousands, and even perhaps millions, of industrious cultivators. It was a completely un- realistic attitude, for, as a Toronto newspaper, which had previously championed the Red River half-castes, bluntly asserted: 'they could be no more successful than Mrs Partington in her well-known effort to brush back the Atlantic tide with a mop and pail'.

Nevertheless, Riel and his followers created a very tense and difficult situation which might well have flared up into a large-scale civil conflict. Fortunately, a man of great deter- mination, strength of character, and persuasiveness was appointed to arbitrate in the dispute. Donald A. Smith had joined the Hudson's Bay Company in 1838 as a junior clerk and, over the years, had made a name for himself as a shrewd and successful fur trader. On the outbreak of the Riel Rebellion, the Governor of Canada sent him to reason with the people of the colony. This he did to such good purpose that they were won over to more moderate ways of thinking. The position of the rebels being largely undermined, they fled across the frontier into the U.S.A., and a peaceful settlement was there- upon arranged.

As a result of that fantastic incident, Donald A. Smith became very much of a public figure. In due course he rose to fill the position that such distinguished persons as Prince Rupert, the Duke of York (afterwards King James II), and the Duke of Marlborough had held before him—the Governorship of the Hudson's Bay Company. He was elected to the office in 1889 and retained it for twenty-five years. In 1897 he was raised to the peerage as Baron Strathcona, and continued to be active in many different spheres until he died, in January 1914, at the age of ninety-three.

When the First World War broke out in August of that year the Hudson's Bay Company was appointed purchasing agent for the French Government, and in the period 1914–1919 handled many millions of tons of essential supplies. It operated a large mercantile fleet which transported cargoes of timber, wood-pulp, coal, sugar, breadstuffs and ground-nuts to France from Argentine, Australia, the U.S.A., West Africa, Morocco, Canada, the Baltic, Cuba, Java, England, and many other countries. One of the Company's ships, the S.S. *Nascopie*, distinguished itself by sinking a German submarine off the Russian coast.

The capital resources of the Hudson's Bay Company, which stood at a modest £10,500 in 1670, had necessarily to be increased and reorganized on a number of occasions. It was trebled, as we have seen, in 1690, and again in 1720; today, when the tercentenary is about to be celebrated, over £13,000,000 are employed in the business. Supplemental charters were granted to the Company on eight separate occasions between 1884 and 1963 to meet altered internal and external conditions. The stock was converted into shares, which are quoted on the London Stock Exchange and may be purchased by anyone, king or commoner, who has the means to buy.

The headquarters of the Hudson's Bay Company, which holds the distinction of being Britain's oldest chartered trading organization, remains in London: at Beaver House, Great Trinity Lane, E.C.4., where the Governor and Committee meet at regular intervals and the periodic fur-auctions are still held.

* 9 *

The South Sea Company

SPAIN, prior to 1469, had been a weak, divided country, part of it still occupied by alien conquerors. In that year, however, Ferdinand V of Castile married his cousin Isabella of Aragon, and a few years later the two Spanish kingdoms were for the first time united under a single rule. When the Moors were driven out of Granada in 1492 Spain entered into the most remarkable and brilliant period of her history. After the voyages of Columbus, made possible by Ferdinand's aid and encouragement, Spain gradually became mistress of an empire exceeding in size and potential wealth that of any other European state. Her most important prizes were, of course, Central and South America, where her culture and language have remained dominant to the present day.

Though the power of Spain declined after the defeat of the Armada in 1588, she clung tenaciously to her conquests and jealously guarded her overseas trade, passing laws and imposing heavy duties with the object of excluding foreign merchants from her colonies. This ban was in full force early in the eighteenth century, when the formation of a company trading to the 'South Seas' was being considered by a group of London projectors. However, like most laws and prohibitions, it left loopholes, and was evaded by various subterfuges. One of the most commonly adopted by English merchants was to consign goods in the names of Spanish subjects—sending them 'coloured' as it was called. Another method frequently employed was to sell goods to Spaniards, payment being made to the English suppliers on successful conclusion of the ventures. Yet a third device was to lend money to Spanish merchants,

who used it to send galleons to the New World, repayment
being made on their safe return. All three methods involved
considerable risk.

II

Proposals for the formation of a company to trade with the
Spanish West Indies—Cuba, Hispaniola, Puerto Rico—had
been made a century earlier, but without result. The suggestion,
however, was revived soon after the outbreak, in 1701, of the
War of the Spanish Succession, when England and other
nations challenged Loius XIV of France over a dynastic issue
in which the Spanish throne was involved. Fresh prospects
were then opened—especially after the French defeats at
Blenheim and Malplaquet—of profitable trade with the Spanish
colonies. That trade, in the opinion of many a staid London
merchant, looking round for new worlds to conquer, appeared
as the one glittering prize that the successful outcome of the
war would bring within the English grasp.

Shortly after the return of a new, Tory Government to
power in 1710, the setting up of a South Sea Company was
being actively discussed, not only among the merchants and
professional company promoters but by leading politicians.
Secret peace negotiations were in progress when, in September
1710, a Bill was hastily passed by the House of Commons
authorising the Company's incorporation. Organised on a joint
stock basis, and entitled 'The Governor and Company of the
Merchants of Great Britain trading to the South Seas and other
parts of America, and for encouraging the Fishing' it was
granted the monopoly, from 1st August, 1711, of trade 'into and
from the lands of South America, from the river Orinoco to
the southernmost part of Tierra del Fuego, and from the said
southernmost part through the South Seas and along the west
coast to the northernmost part of America, and into and from
all countries within those limits, reputed to belong to the
Crown of Spain, and other countries hereafter to be discovered'.

With such a grandiose concession, in a part of the world
believed to be a veritable Eldorado, no one doubted that a
brilliant future lay before the new corporation. However,

there were from the very beginning certain unusual features about the South Sea Company, arising from the fact that it was a 'hybrid', i.e. partly a trading company, like the East India Company, and partly a financial institution, like the Bank of England—for one of its main purposes was to help the Government overcome certain acute and pressing financial difficulties. These had been caused, at least in part, by the refusal of the Whig merchants, who dominated both the East India Company and the Bank, to lend money to an administration made up of their political rivals. The South Sea Company's directors, in exchange for their monopolistic priviliges, had promised nothing less than to take over some £9,500,000 of the public debt!

The essence of the scheme was that owners of Government securities were to be invited to exchange them for South Sea Company stock. Since many of the securities involved had fallen far below their nominal value, while the stock was confidently expected to rise, the offer was not without its attractions, and it was believed that there would be an overwhelmingly favourable response.

That optimistic appraisal of the situation proved, in the event, to be correct. There was a rush to support the Company; and though the City remained divided, a whole new tribe of popular journalists hailed the South Sea scheme as a masterly blend of commerce and finance, which would benefit not only a small minority but the entire nation.

III

Even in those early days of euphoria, however, warning voices were raised—as, for example, that of Daniel Defoe, who laid his finger on the fundamental instability of the foundations on which the Company had been set up when he pointed out that, unless the Spaniards were utterly devoid of commonsense and bent on their own ruin, they could not possibly 'part with so valuable, indeed so inestimable, a jewel as the exclusive power of trade to their own plantations'.

No one listened, however, and by the time that the formal

charter of incorporation was granted to the Company, on 10th September, 1711, thousands of holders of Government securities had accepted the conversion offer. Among the subscribers for stock were some of the wealthiest men in the country—and heartening support came from financiers and bankers on the continent. Robert Harley, Earl of Oxford, chief minister at the time, was appointed first Governor, with support from a sub-Governor, a Deputy-Governor, and a Court of thirty directors. The Company acquired a coat of arms, in which appeared the motto *From Cadiz to the Dawn*, and a suitably imposing building was rented as a head office. Officials—including a secretary, an accountant, and a cashier —were appointed, and everything was ready for action.

To all outward appearances the South Sea Company was a substantial, wealthy and highly respectable concern—a worthy compeer of the East India Company and of the Bank of England; indeed there were those who thought it ranked high above those two august and respected institutions. As the War of the Spanish Succession approached its victorious end, hopes rose high that a profitable trade with South America would soon begin. The directors began to busy themselves with the preparation of long inventories of British goods— ranging from sealing-wax to worsted hose, from Cheshire cheese to watches and clocks—which it was proposed to export. The slave trade, too, it was predicted, would soar to unprecedented heights.

Unfortunately, when the Treaty of Utrecht was signed in 1713, and peace came, the result, from the South Sea Company's point of view, fell a great deal short of its expectations. King Philip did, in fact, confer on England the right to send 4,800 negroes annually to the Spanish-American colonies. Under this agreement, known as the Assiento Pact and valid for thirty years, the Company was furthermore allowed to set up establishments at Buenos Aires, Caracas, Havana, Vera Cruz and several other ports. There was disappointment, however, when it was learnt that the Spaniards would allow only one ship annually to sail for purposes of general trade. Even that derisory concession was subject to the proviso that the King of Spain would receive one-quarter of the profits of each voyage.

It was then that the directors, becoming all too painfully aware that the Company's complex organization and huge capital resources were incommensurate with its limited trading opportunities, took the turning that was to bring about one of the most fearful economic and social disasters in British history.

IV

The South Sea Company was, as we have seen, something of a hybrid—a dichotomous entity which, from the outset, had been expected to function both as a legitimate commercial venture and as a Government debt-absorbing agency. Foiled in its attempts to establish a trading empire, as the East India Company was in process of doing, it sought to outshine the Bank of England by a further, and even more ambitious, excursion into the realm of State finance.

Late in the year 1719, when under the domination of a forceful, overbearing and unscrupulous director, the Company adumbrated and put forward a scheme for taking over the National Debt in its entirety! John Blount and his friends —the word 'accomplices' is as yet a little premature—envisaged another grand conversion operation. The National Debt, which comprised the annuities (sold to finance the war against France) and some miscellaneous obligations—amounted to the then unprecedented amount of £50 million, and the plan was to invite holders of Government securities to exchange them for South Sea Company stock. In return, the Government was to pay interest to the Company (though at a lower rate than it was paying to the security holders), to pay management expenses, and to grant the Company a monopoly of world-trade—European trade only being excluded.

Neither the abstruse complexities of the scheme, nor the modifications that had to be made before the Government accepted it, need be described. To grasp what was going on in the minds of John Blount and his associates it is necessary to understand only one thing: by a whirlwind of propaganda the value of South Sea stock was to be artificially hoisted to far above its real value. An illusion of limitless wealth was to be created, which would not only ensure an enthusiastic response to the conversion offer, but enable the Debt securities to be snapped up cheaply—for though the stock would be made to soar the securities could never rise above par.

The first symptoms of South Sea fever appeared in the early summer of 1720—'shipwreck year' as the historian Gibbon was later to describe it. Both Houses of Parliament had, by large majorities, approved the South Sea Company's proposals in April, but the upward movement in the market price of stock had begun before that. In February stock had been purchased in large blocks at 160; in March it was commanding 184; on 7th April, after King George I (who was also Governor of the Company) gave his assent to the Parliamentary Bill, it touched 335, and even that was no more than a prelude to the spectacular and rip-roaring boom that lay ahead.

V

The centre to which all who dreamt of making a fortune in Bubble year automatically gravitated was Change Alley, in the heart of the City; and contemporary accounts of the incredible scenes witnessed there make fascinating reading. People from every walk of life were drawn into the narrow space between Lombard Street and Cornhill; for there—in the two Coffee Houses, Garraways and Jonathans—the stock-jobbers, who brought buyers into contact with sellers, were to be found.

Everyone with money to burn made ready for a gamble in South Sea stock, or if not South Sea then some other likely stock. For the pressure of demand built up to such an extent that it spilled over to include a whole host of other companies, mushroom growths for the greater part, who were as lavish in their promises as implausible in their purposes. John Blount regarded these 'minor bubbles' as not only a nuisance but a menace, and their suppression by Act of Parliament was largely due to his protests. Meantime, he had the satisfaction of seeing South Sea stock soar in less than a month from 800 to 1,050, and that figure, reached on 30th June, marked the peak-point beyond which a gullible public refused to go.

A few weeks later Blount, after the king had honoured him with a baronetcy, departed for a much-needed holiday to Tunbridge Wells, and while there decided that the time had come to dispose of at least part of his own substantial holding of South Sea stock. Before mid-August, the market price had fallen to 900, and towards the end of the month the tide was ebbing fast. On 1st September sellers were still able to unload their holdings at 770, but suddenly everyone was afraid. Panic selling then sent the price tumbling headlong—to 575, 380, 150—until, finally, the stock was virtually unsaleable at any price.

So great was this disaster of the South Sea Bubble that the Government was obliged to intervene. The directors' estates were confiscated, a committee was formed to examine the Company's books of account, and various proposals were considered for restoring 'the public credit'. Sir Robert Walpole —Britain's first prime minister—mitigated the effects of the crash as best he could. To do full justice to those who had been swindled and forced into bankruptcy was, of course, impossible —and the situation brought about by the midsummer madness of 1720 was accepted as irreversible. The losers remained the losers, and had no alternative but to adjust to their altered circumstances—unless, indeed, they preferred to blow out their brains, which many did.

VI

Most of the leading figures who had bewitched and bemused the country with their tales of gold and silver mines in South America gradually disappeared from the scene, by escaping abroad, by withdrawing into discreet retirement, or by dying. The South Sea Company itself, however, managed to survive the crisis. As a financial institution it was, of course, thoroughly discredited, but there still remained a reasonable prospect that it might succeed in the overseas trade, and in the 'Fishing' which had been mentioned in the charter as one of its objects.

The Assiento Pact had still over twenty years to run, and the slave trade, therefore, was continued—notwithstanding that in earlier years it had failed to produce any significant profits. Like its competitor the Royal African Company, the South Sea Company found that losses due to the high death rate among the slaves, the multifarious charges, imposts, duties and expenses made far deeper inroads into gross receipts than had been anticipated. Muddle and managerial incompetence, and illicit trading by the Company's employees, were further contributory causes of failure. This pattern, established in the years prior to 1720, persisted even after the reconstruction.

The Greenland whale-fishing had been of some importance since the time of Queen Elizabeth who, in 1577, had granted the Russia Company sole rights for a period of twenty years. During the Civil War, and under the Commonwealth, men had to be withdrawn from the whaling-fleets and the trade virtually came to an end. After various efforts had been made to revive it, the trade was thrown open. That was in 1702—but no great interest was shown until the formation of the South Sea Company nine years later. Between 1724 and 1732 the directors channelled a great deal of capital into the whale fisheries, all to no purpose—for losses of £178,000 had to be written off.

A fleet of twenty-three ships fitted out in 1728 returned with the blubber and fins of only eighteen whales—which could by no stretch of the imagination be described as a profitable voyage. Yet it was typical, and so, in due course, the Company was obliged to abandon its attempts to 'improve the Fishing', and relinquish its privileges in favour of other adventurers who, with more determination and skill, were able to make handsome profits.

VII

This lack of success in the slave trade and the whalefisheries was matched by dismal failure of the annual trading venture to South America which the Treaty of Utrecht had specifically provided for. The 'permission ships' should at least have made some modest contribution to the Company's revenues, but here again there was ineptitude, clumsiness and lack of business flair. Cargoes of woollen goods, for example, were sent to markets already overstocked, while other markets existed nearby where textiles of all kinds were in short supply.

There were other difficulties, arising from the fact that governments in the seventeenth century tended to regard companies as milch-cows to whom recourse could be had not only for loans in national emergency, but whenever a little extra money was needed. Charters were granted or renewed only on condition of massive loans or contributions to the Exchequer, and there were other 'rake-offs' in the form of special levies, commissions and bribes. Philip, King of Spain, under the Treaty of Utrecht had reserved for himself 25 per cent of the profits made on each annual voyage. Queen Anne, in 1714, tried to obtain a similar percentage for herself, and though the demand had to be withdrawn, it gave the directors an unpleasant shock. Many other tributes continued, however, to be remorsely exacted.

Two other evils with which the South Sea Company had to contend were the obstructive tactics adopted by the Spanish-American authorities, in delaying and detaining its ships and withholding sailing licences, and the practice, apparently insuppressible, of the ships' captains and officers from taking cargoes aboard for personal trading. These and other abuses multiplied so fast, and were so disheartening, that the directors were forced to consider discontinuing the trade.

The last permission ship, the *Royal Caroline*, actually sailed in 1730, laden with goods that were intended for the Porto-Bello fair. The Spaniards, however, delayed the ship so that their own galleons should arrive in the Caribbean first. Three years later, after a long detention in the Mexican port of Vera Cruz, the *Royal Caroline* returned to England with a rich cargo of cochineal, indigo and pieces of eight (Spanish dollars). The extraordinary thing about this particular venture was that it resulted in a profit of £70,000, and therefore stands out in the Company's history as its one brilliant and successful trading coup.

So while the East India Company and the Bank of England were rapidly extending the scope of their activities, the South Sea Company—which in 1720 had schemed and plotted to overthrow both—only just managed to keep its head above

9. Cecil Rhodes, by
G. F. Watts.

(*National Portrait Gallery*)

10. Robert Clive, by
N. Dance.

(*National Portrait Gallery*)

11. Groote Schuur, Capetown. (*Mansell Collection*)

12. Johannesburg, 1891. (*Mansell Collection*)

13. Sir George Goldie, 1899, by H. von Herkomer.

(*National Portrait Gallery*)

14. Lord Lugard, by Pilkington Jackson.

(*National Portrait Gallery*)

15. Sir James Brooke,
Rajah of Sarawak.

(*Mansell Collection*)

16. Loading wool at Carcass Island, Falkland Islands.

(*By courtesy of the Falkland Islands Company*)

water. Never for one moment, however, did those in command of its destinies abandon their dream of exploiting the fabled riches of South America and the South Seas—until 1750, when the Company had to surrender its privileges under the Assiento pact. The Spaniards compensated the Company with a lump-sum payment of £100,000, and thereafter it was left with only one non-trading function—i.e. to collect the annuity it received from the Government on part of the National Debt, and to distribute that annuity in the form of dividends to stockholders.

VIII

More decades passed during which the Company dragged out some kind of existence, though to all intents and purposes it was defunct. South Sea House, a handsome three-storey building in Threadneedle Street, was retained as a headquarters, and the sort of place it was in the Company's twilight days is vividly described by Charles Lamb in one of his most evocative essays.

'This was once a house of trade', he wrote in *The South Sea House*, 'a centre of busy interests. The throng of merchants was here—the quick pulse of gain—and here some forms of business are still kept up, though the soul be long since fled'.

Lamb had been employed as a junior clerk in South Sea House in the 1790s, and writes nostalgically of the friends and acquaintances he made there. It was during his lifetime, in 1807, that the Company was at long last deprived of the trading privileges which, under Queen Anne's charter, it still retained. Even that was not the *coup de grace*, and it was left to a Victorian prime minister to effect the final winding up of its affairs.

The South Sea Company in 1854 still had a capital of £10,000,000, which Mr Gladstone converted into Consols and reintegrated into the National Debt, where it properly belonged. So the absurd, melancholy and yet strangely fascinating saga ended.

* 10 *

Royal Adventurers into Africa

THE interest of European traders in the 'dark continent' of Africa is of very old standing, and takes us back at least five hundred years. Much of the pioneering work was done by the Portuguese, but the English adventurers were early in the field. When, for example, the King of Portugal captured Ceuta in 1415, it would appear that he was actively aided by merchants from this country.

Portuguese sovereignty, during the same century, came to be extended to considerable portions of Africa—though mainly on the coast. By 1480, the navigators were familiar with the shores of Guinea; in 1482 a certain Diogo Cam entered the mouth of the lordly Niger, and with the rounding of the Cape of Good Hope, by Bartholomew Diaz in 1488, African geography was beginning to be well understood.

The principal trade indulged in by the Portuguese was in such commodities as pepper, ivory and gold—of which last mentioned large alluvial deposits had been found. With the discovery of America, by Columbus in 1492, the slave trade, which had for long been carried on by the Arabs of North Africa, assumed a position of great importance, for it was extremely lucrative; so much so, that it excited the envy of other countries, and the Portuguese monopoly was soon challenged.

II

One of the earliest British voyagers to the west coast of Africa was William Hawkins, father of Sir John Hawkins, who visited Guinea in 1530; and there were trading expeditions, of which records have been kept, to Barbary twenty-one years later. In 1553, a *Company of Merchant Adventurers for Guinea* was formed, on a joint stock basis.

They organized several voyages, and were a body of legitimate traders, who won the confidence of the natives to a remarkable degree, by refraining from any dealings in the slave traffic, which was largely in the hands of the Portuguese at that stage, causing them to be both hated and feared. The Adventurers for Guinea returned from their second voyage, according to Hakluyt, with considerable quantities of gold 'of two and twenty carats and one grain in fineness, and about two hundred and fifty elephants' teeth of all kinds, some of nine spans in length and big as a man's thigh above the knee'.

The standing of this early group of adventurers is vouched for by the fact that in 1561 Queen Elizabeth was pleased to be admitted as a partner or stockholder. She provided four ships, and spent the sum of £500 in provisioning them for a voyage. Goods for trading purposes, valued at £5,000 were supplied by other members of the Company, and the agreement was that the profits realised were to be divided into three parts, of which the Queen was to receive one.

In the following year another expedition was organized with a formal agreement, which took the form of an Indenture and Charter Party under the Great Seal, and one assumes from this that Elizabeth was satisfied with her adventure in the first. On this second occasion she spent a certain amount of money in equipping the vessels, and undertook to provide gunners, sailors and pilots. That she was a capable business woman is proved by the fact that she expressly forbade private trading by members of the expedition, and also stipulated that the accounts should be subject to audit.

All these early enterprises would appear to have yielded satisfactory results, despite the harassments of the Portuguese, which often resulted in brisk skirmishes at sea. A great deal of this initial success must undoubtedly be attributed to the confidence which the natives reposed in the English traders, whom they actually came to regard as allies against their Portuguese oppressors.

This goodwill was dispersed at a single blow by Sir John

Hawkins who, hearing of the fabulous prices to be obtained
for slaves in Hispaniola—that is, the West Indies—sailed for
the Guinea coast and abducted some 300 negroes for transportation. Hawkins's raid took place in 1562, and Hakluyt
mentions five persons, together with others not named but
probably sub-shareholders, who were associated with him
in financing this first entry into a notorious and barbaric
trafficking in human beings.

The extreme profitability of slave trading can be gathered
from the result of the Hawkins venture. Arriving in the West
Indies with his cargo, he made rapid sales—for, owing to the
slow extermination of the native population of the islands,
labour was scarce—and with the proceeds purchased hides,
sugar and ginger in such quantities that the holds were filled
to capacity, and he was obliged to purchase two more ships to
carry home the surplus.

The contradictory position which resulted in Africa, is
aptly summarised by W. R. Scott (*Joint Stock Companies to 1720*)
in the following passage:

> 'Once Hawkins had raided the coast, two sets of English-
> men were working by contrary methods: the original
> Adventurers were simply traders, whilst Hawkins was mainly
> engaged in capturing slaves. It was inevitable that the
> presence of the latter, by alarming the natives, destroyed the
> chances of the former . . .'

Other early groups of English adventurers were formed,
but it is impossible to devote much space to their activities.
The *Senegal Adventurers* were chartered in 1588, and were
granted sole rights of trading in the territory situated between
the Senegal River and Gambia, for a period of ten years.

James I granted a charter to another group which had come
into existence round the personality of Sir William St. John,
the builder of a fort on the African coast. This body, *The
Governor and Company of Adventurers of London trading to Gynney
and Bynney*, was incorporated in 1618, with 'perpetual succession
and a common seal'. Nevertheless, it was extremely short-lived,
the span of its existence running to only six years.

Yet another Company of Merchants trading to Guinea was

formed a little later, but ran heavily into debt, and maintained a precarious existence until the time of the Restoration, when *The Company of Royal Adventurers trading into Africa* stepped into its shoes. This company, incorporated by royal charter in 1660 by Charles II, conferred rights of exclusive trade along the entire African coast from Sallee to the Cape of Good Hope, and was patronized by some of the most distinguished people in the country.

Prince Rupert was its first Governor, and his thirty-six colleagues or 'assistants' included other men of title.

III

At first the Royal Adventurers appear to have prospered in their affairs, but presently ran into trouble when they attacked the forts of their rivals, the Dutch traders, who had by then arrived on the African coast. Belligerent acts of this kind naturally provoked retaliation, and we find the Dutch raiding the English forts in 1665, and robbing the Royal Adventurers of their stock-in-trade.

This conflict with the Dutch merchants brought about a serious deterioration in the trade, and the Company soon found itself in financial difficulties. The Governor and his assistants, tried to farm out the African trade to outsiders. In 1668 they actually received an offer of £1,000 per annum for seven years, and apparently accepted this miserable rent for the privileges that were theirs under the charter. Those privileges included, as we have seen, the right to trade along the whole of the known African coast—with the gold hills of Bambuk, and the fabled riches of Timbuctu, in the hinterland.

The financial difficulties of the Royal Adventurers were undoubtedly severe. Not only were the meagre rents totally inadequate to meet the company's obligations to creditors, but the situation was further aggravated by the failure of many of the adventurers, including the king himself, to take up their shares. A winding-up and the surrender of the charter became inevitable in order that a suggested scheme of arrangement could be carried out. The debts amounted to £57,000, a large sum of money at that time, while the assets were negligible, apart from the charter itself. That indeed had some potential value, but until fresh working capital was forthcoming, it signified little—and no one could be expected to provide such capital so long as the existing load of indebtedness hung like a millstone round the company's neck.

The full story of the reconstruction is too long to be told here, but in essence it was quite simple: after the winding-up of the old company a new one was to be formed, in which both members and creditors were to be incorporated.

A drastic writing down of the capital was involved, nine-tenths of it having been irretrievably lost. The creditors had their debts discharged by an allocation of stock of the old company, being two-thirds of the amount owing to them, and they could exchange this for a smaller amount of the new stock. The net result was that they suffered a ninety per-cent reduction, except for the remaining one third of the indebtedness, which was to be satisfied in cash out of the proceeds of a new sub-scription.

Agreement having been reached on all essential points, King Charles was called upon to sanction the scheme, and to give his blessing to the *Royal African Company*, as this second company was called. It started off with a capital of £100,000, and the charter of 1672 confirmed its right to trade from Sallee to the Cape of Good Hope and the adjacent islands. Further, the company was entitled to acquire lands not owned by any other Christian prince 'to have and to hold for one thousand years, subject to the payment of two elephants' teeth' whenever any member of the royal family landed on African soil.

IV

The monopoly granted to the Royal African Company was intended to be of a more watertight character than that of its predecessors had been. No English subject was to visit west Africa for trading purposes except by permission of the company, which was empowered to seize the ships and goods of would-be free-traders. To make the restrictions even more effective, the English customs were ordered to keep an eye on all exports to and imports from west African ports. Finally, the company was authorised to set up a Court on the African coast to deal with interlopers on the spot. This was a unique privilege which, at that time, not even the mighty East India Company enjoyed.

One of the principal objects of the company was the mining of gold and silver, but specific mention is made in the charter of negroes. In fact, the buying and selling of slaves developed into a major activity and source of profit. As early as 1674 the company had a settlement at Ophra on the Slave Coast and one of the factors, Thomas Clarke, reported home that 'six or seven thousand slaves could be purchased' without difficulty every year. Later Ophra was abandoned in favour of Whydah, where a factory or depot was established.

At Whydah in 1683 a negro slave could be bought for English goods to the value of two or three pounds, but prices varied at different times and on different parts of the coast. A high proportion of the trade was conducted with minor chieftains in the Niger delta and at the mouths of other rivers. The slaves themselves were transported from the interior, many of them being prisoners-of-war taken in tribal conflicts, criminals or debtors, but others were simply the victims of organized raids.

Herded into the slaving ships like cattle, they were taken across the Atlantic to the West Indies, where labour was desperately needed on the sugar plantations. The mortality rate on the 'middle passage' was never less than five per-cent and more usually twenty per-cent. On one quite disastrous voyage in a ship named the *Francis*, 199 out of 267 slaves were lost. Many, of course, were in poor condition or actually suffering from disease at the time of embarkation. Still, the toll from overcrowding, and brutality on the part of ships' captains, was heavy. The strong or fortunate ones who survived their ordeal could be sold in Barbados for £15, in Jamaica for £17, and in Virginia for £18 a head!

Overall, it has been estimated that between 1673 and 1711 the Royal African Company delivered more than 90,000 slaves to the British West Indies, but the actual figure is not known and may well be larger. Towards the end of the period, however, there was an appreciable slackening off in the traffic. Yet it was not until 1807 that, as a result of humanitarian agitation, slave-trading in all British dominions was prohibited.

By way of footnote, it may be mentioned that the company's employees in Africa found themselves in a predicament almost as appalling as that of the slaves—for the west coast was then the 'white man's grave'. Disease was rampant, and the average expectation of life in and around the forts was seldom more than five or six years.

V

An interesting point may be noted in connection with the Royal African Company—it had a Governor, a sub-Governor, a Deputy-Governor, and twenty-four assistants. The unusual office of *sub*-Governor is accounted for by the fact that the governorship of the company was an honorary position, usually held by a member of the royal family, while the sub-Governor was the person on whose shoulders the actual day-to-day management of affairs devolved. The capital, as already stated, was £100,000, and each holding of £500 carried with it one vote.

For seven years after the incorporation of the Royal African Company, excellent results were recorded. For the three years 1676–1678 the dividends were as high as 55 per-cent. In 1691 the fortunate stockholders participated in a bonus issue, as a result of which their original capital was increased fourfold.

As the seventeenth century drew to its close, however, the company faced a succession of lean years. The causes were twofold: first, the trade with west Africa was disorganized by war; secondly, the illicit activities of the English interlopers, or independents, had reached high proportions.

These were the same merchants and traders, on the whole, who had been attacking the East India Company with its envied monopoly position. Their main tactic was to press for the conversion of the Royal African Company from a joint stock to a regulated corporation. They wanted the doors of the west African trade to be thrown open, and the company to be operated in such a way that each member provided his own capital, pocketed his own profits and bore his own losses.

This issue came to a head in 1690, when Parliament instructed a committee to look into the merits of the controversy.

The company argued that the building and maintenance of forts on the coast necessitated the employment of such large sums as to be beyond the capacity of any single individual, or even body of individuals acting separately, and only available through a joint-stock corporation.

The committee pronounced in favour of a regulated company, as urged by the interlopers, and at last, in 1698, a breach was made in the Royal African Company's defences. An Act was passed by Parliament which recognized the importance of the forts, but permitted all who wished to participate in the west African commerce to do so, on payment to the company of a duty of ten per-cent on all imports and exports.

Early in the eighteenth century, a strenuous effort was made by the Royal African Company to recover the full privileges it had enjoyed under Charles's charter—urging the impossibility of maintaining the forts with the tolls levied on 'precarious traders'—but without success. Again, in 1748, it pressed its claims with utmost resolution, petitioning for the restoration of its monopoly and for the principle of a joint-stock to be recognized.

The traders in the outports, particularly those in Liverpool, opposed these claims with all the means at their disposal. Manchester entered the lists as one of the champions of free trade, roundly condemning monopolies as 'unnatural and unreasonable'.

Out of this controversy came the Act of 1750, which re-affirmed the principle of the regulated as against the joint-stock company; and the traders to Africa were, in fact, prohibited from trading in a corporate capacity. Shortly afterwards, the Royal African Company was wound up and supplanted by a new company, which carried on for nearly seventy years until, in 1821, it too was dissolved.

VI

Something must now be said about the way in which the Royal African Company was administered and controlled from its London offices. The constitution of the company—with a Governor, sub-Governor, Deputy Governor, and a Court of twenty-four assistants—has already been referred to. Election of these principal officers took place annually at the general meetings of the shareholders. Voting rights, not specifically mentioned in the charter of 1672, were at first on the basis of one vote for every £100 of stock, but seem to have been variable at discretion.

The company's prospectus—or 'preamble' as it was called —provided, among other things, that two General Courts were to be convened every year; one to elect officers and another to consider and pass the accounts. Authority for managing the company's affairs, though nominally vested in the General Court, was in practice exercised by the assistants or a committee of the assistants—except on matters of the weightiest kind, to decide which extraordinary meetings of all the members would be held.

The election of a Governor for the Royal African Company was between 1672 and 1685 always a pure formality—for James, the king's brother, was chosen with unfailing regularity. His fortunes and those of the company were, indeed, closely intertwined, and when, after the Revolution of 1688, he was forced to flee the country, the company too suffered a disastrous political defeat. Later, the patronage of William III, Queen Anne and George I was obtained, but all signally failed to identify themselves with the African traders in the way that James had done, first as Duke of York and then as king.

Most of the assistants were merchants and men of wide business experience. In that respect the Royal African Company differed from the Royal Adventurers, whose control had been in the hands of the royal family, peers of the realm, and courtiers. Hence, it has been held, the failure of their venture into commerce and finance!

African House, the London headquarters of the Royal African Company, was originally in Throcmorton Street, and at the height of the company's prosperity some twenty paid officials were employed there. In 1678 a move was made to premises in Leadenhall Street where, to judge from the much higher rent paid, accommodation must have been of a more stately kind.

Among the permanent officials of the company were a

treasurer, a secretary, and an accountant, who all received the same salary—namely, £100 a year, for which they had to work very hard.

VII

Early trade with the west coast of Africa was mainly concerned with the exchange of English goods for gold, ivory, spices, and redwood dyes. The buccaneering exploits of Hawkins have been touched upon as embarrassments to the legitimate traders. After the Restoration all this was altered, and such moral scruples as there had been were swept aside. The west African trade became increasingly to be identified with the traffic in negro slaves to the West Indian sugar and cotton plantations. And the African Company, in the several incarnations to which we have alluded, was implicated up to the hilt, for it derived a great deal of its profits from that source.

However, in fairness it must be added that, in relation to the slave trade as a whole, the activities of the English adventurers, which are comparatively well-documented, were of somewhat less significance than is generally thought. French, Portuguese, Dutch and Spanish traders were also involved in large-scale operations. The shipments of slaves to Brazil and Cuba were particularly heavy, though statistics and literature on the subject are almost completely lacking. Recent demographic studies, however, lead to the conclusion that as many as *fifteen million* Africans found their way across the Atlantic to the various European colonies. This puts the figure of 90,000, quoted above as the English share of the trade, into a more favourable perspective, and suggests that though we were in bad company our traders were perhaps less culpable than those of some other countries. The whole subject, however, remains very controversial.

Though the London traders played a prominent part in the traffic, those of Liverpool were not far behind, for during the eighteenth century there was a close connection between the slave trade and the Lancashire cotton industry. Vessels were despatched from the north-country port with finished cotton goods, which were sold at good prices to the West African natives. The traders would then take on board cargoes of slaves, cross the Atlantic and make their deals with the plantation owners, and finally return to Liverpool with shipments of tobacco, sugar and raw cotton. A profit was made (in the absence of untoward circumstances) at each of the three separate stages.

However, as the nineteenth century dawned the public conscience became uneasy about the matter, and the Government was persuaded to act. In 1807 the traffic, which by then had become less profitable, was declared illegal, and the Royal Navy was given the task of stopping it in all British territories.

From that point onwards the West African trade began to develop along quite different lines. The interior of the continent, hitherto somewhat neglected, began to be explored. Gold deposits were discovered in Ashanti; Nigeria was penetrated, and the entire region found to be a rich source of raw materials and of foodstuffs. The most important natural product was, perhaps, the palm oil from which margarine and soap are manufactured, and on which a great Anglo-Dutch industrial empire has since been built up.

* 11 *

The Royal Niger Company

TWO of the great chartered companies dealt with in earlier chapters—the Royal African Company and the South Sea Company—had been deeply implicated in the West African slave trade but had not found it altogether profitable. When, in 1807, humanitarian agitation in England forced the prohibition of the slave trade (and in 1833 of slave holding) interest shifted to the infinite natural riches of the 'Dark Continent', which included not only gold, ivory and indigo but palm oil, used in the manufacture of margarine and soap.

Little, however, was known about the vast hinterlands, except that they were, for the white man, very unhealthy. The African interior, therefore remained *terra incognita* until it was discovered that the parasites causing malaria could be effectively controlled by quinine. The Scottish explorer Mungo Park had, it is true, followed the inland course of the Niger, Africa's third longest river, as far back as 1795–7, and again in 1805–6, but without finding either its source or its various mouths in the delta. These remained mysteries that were not solved until much later in the nineteenth century.

One of the first trading ventures into the Niger valley was that of M. Laird and R. Lander who, having formed a company, equipped two small steamers and sailed up the river in 1832. They reached Nupe, on the lower Niger, and gained much useful knowledge concerning the native customs, political alignments, religion and trade. Unfortunately, disease levied a dreadful toll, for thirty-nine out of forty-eight of those taking part in the venture died. The Niger Expedition of 1841, though on a larger scale, fared little better—indeed, suffered such alarming casualties that further surveys were discouraged for over a decade. Trade between the African interior and the European traders was conducted almost entirely through a powerful body of middlemen, who lived on the coast.

Later, in the 1850s, William Balfour Baikie and others were more successful. With the aid of quinine, the mortality rate due to malaria was greatly reduced, and it became possible to explore the lands on either side of the lordly Niger with fair hopes of survival. After that important break-through, a regular and direct trade between British traders and the interior, by-passing the middlemen, was gradually developed.

II

The year 1876 saw the formation of the Central African Trading Company, of which George Goldie, one of the more vital figures in the making of Nigeria, was a director. A man of boundless energy, he embarked on a policy aimed at eliminating the fierce competition which had by that time sprung up in the Niger trade. Tireless effort on his part, over a long period, eventually resulted in formation of the United African Company, which brought together the assets and rights of a number of rival firms on the river. It was this company, incorporated with limited liability in November 1879, that was later to be reorganized as the National African Company and to receive a royal charter. Though the Government's attitude to the new corporation was ambivalent and vacillating, it was generally regarded as an instrument of Britain's commercial and political interests in a part of the world where the scramble for colonies was becoming fast and furious. France had already established a protectorate over Dahomey; the Germans had grabbed the Cameroons; and both had their designs on those regions of the Niger on which the British hold was as yet tenuous and insecure.

Sealed on 10th July, 1886, Queen Victoria's charter confirmed the objects of the National African Company—it was not called the Royal Niger Company until later—as they had been stated in 1882, when the Company had first been registered. Among other things, the directors were (a) empowered to act as merchants, bankers or traders, shipowners and carriers, (b) to form or acquire and carry on trading stations, factories, stores and depots in Africa, (c) to enter into treaties for the granting of privileges, monopolies, concessions to the Company by African potentates or rulers, (d) to stock, cultivate and improve Company lands and erect buildings thereon, and (f) to do all other things whatsoever in any way incidental or conducive to the foregoing objects. The capital was £1,000,000, divided into 100,000 shares of £10 each, with power to increase.

The charter goes on sonorously to declare:

And whereas the Petitioner [i.e. the Company] further states that the Kings, Chiefs, and peoples of various territories in the basin of the River Niger, in Africa, fully recognizing after many years' experience, the benefits accorded to their country by their intercourse with the Company and their predecessors, have ceded the whole of their respective territories to the Company by various Acts of Cession specified in the Schedule hereto.

And whereas the Petitioners further state that the Company, since their incorporation, have been actively engaged in carrying into effect the objects stated in the aforesaid Memorandum of Association, and have purchased the businesses of all European traders in the regions aforesaid, and are now the sole European traders there, and are now engaged in developing the resources of such regions and in extending trade further into the interior.

And whereas the Petitioner further states that the Company and their predecessors, whose businesses they purchased, have, during many years past, expended large sums of money and made great exertions in and about acquiring the confidence of the said native Kings, Chiefs, and peoples, which have resulted in the said Cessions of territory . . .

And whereas the Petitioner further states that the condition of the natives inhabiting the aforesaid territories would be materially improved, and the development of such territories and those contiguous thereto, and the civilization of their people would be greatly advanced . . .

And whereas the Petitioner further states that if such

authority [i.e. authority under royal charter to accept the Cessions] were conferred on the Petitioner Company they would thereby be enabled to render to Our Dominions services of much value, and to promote the commercial prosperity of many of Our Subjects.

Now, therefore, We, having taken the said Petition into Our Royal consideration, in our Council, and being satisfied that the intentions of the Petitioner Company are praiseworthy and deserve encouragement, do hereby will, ordain, grant, and declare as follows, that is to say:

The said National African Company Limited . . . is hereby authorized and empowered to hold and retain the full benefit of the several Cessions aforesaid . . . and all rights, interests, authorities, and powers for the purposes of government, preservation of public order . . . and to hold, use, enjoy and exercise the same lands, property, rights, interests, and powers respectively for the purposes of the Company and on the terms of this Our Charter.

It is a comparatively short, lucid document, and the passages quoted are worth reading because of the light they throw on antecedent events.

III

The entry of Germany and France on the West African scene has already been noted. For many years both posed a threat to George Goldie and the Royal Niger Company, whose territorial claims were either disputed or ignored. No less persistent and harassing, however, were the tactics of the Liverpool traders, who had established themselves in the coastal regions. Backed by an influential group of Members of Parliament, they opposed the Company and—like the interlopers of old—maintained that trade should be free and unrestricted.

In the charter it was expressly stated that the Company was not authorised to set up or grant any monopoly of trade, though it could impose customs duties and charges for the purpose of defraying the necessary expenses of government, administering justice and maintaining law and order. Goldie, however, placed his own interpretation on that particular clause, and had firmly decided that only through monopoly, and the exclusion of competitors, could he and the Royal Niger Company succeed in their dual role of empire builders and traders. As the Company was already well entrenched on both sides of the Niger, with stations and recognized property rights, it had no great difficulty in enforcing that policy. However, once it had been embarked upon, a head-on clash with the Liverpool merchants, vitally interested in palm oil for soap-making, became inevitable.

Goldie, a clever diplomat, listened to the Liverpool faction's allegations of misrule, of demoralizing the native Nigerians with gin, of forcing the coastal middlemen out of business, and sundry other abuses, and riposted by suggesting that they should discuss their differences with a view to combining forces. The Liverpool men, in short, were invited to become the Company's 'partners, co-directors, and co-rulers', and by that means eliminate the mad competition that had arisen.

Goldie, in advancing this plan, painted a glowing picture of the prospects before such an enlarged Company—in a region so 'wondrously fertile' and yet underdeveloped and even unexplored. 'We know', he declared, 'that the natural products of this district are boundless and that coffee and cocoa could be more profitably grown than palm oil or palm kernels'.

Conflicting interests, disagreements and hostilities—including the opposition of the shipping lines to an amalgamated company —ruled out any immediate possibility of fusion. The Liverpool traders, in fact, formed their own separate organization—the African Association Limited—and tried to obtain a separate charter to cover the 'Oil Rivers,' i.e. the regions that lay behind the mangrove swamps on either side of the Niger delta, where the palm trees, from the fruit of which the palm oil was obtained, grew wild in the forest belt.

The Association's attempt to obtain a separate charter failed, and its rivalry with the Royal Niger Company, therefore, continued unabated. No settlement was reached until June, 1893, when the Royal Niger Company acquired all the Association's plant, machinery, buildings, produce, and other assets. Spheres of influence were defined—the Association being allowed to predominate on the Oil Rivers, and the Company on the Niger. All competition between the two groups then ceased.

This conclusion was, in a very real sense, a victory for Goldie's policy of control through monopoly and the strict regulation of trade. Certainly after 1893 the commerce, both on the Niger and Benue rivers, was effectively in the Company's hands.

IV

Very closely associated with the palm oil trade, and with the Liverpool merchants, were the 'Brassmen', who occupied the coastal region in and around the Niger delta. The land there was agriculturally unproductive, and they had at first been fishermen, but later turned to the slave trade. When that declined, early in the nineteenth century, they set up as middlemen, through whom the European traders maintained contact with the inhabitants of the interior, and vice versa.

For the Brassmen,* integration of the Liverpool traders into the Royal Niger Company had catastrophic results. During the period of competition between the two groups they had done well—not least by their smuggling activities, which had deprived the Company of considerable sums in duty. Now that Goldie was acknowledged lord and master of the Niger, he was able to suppress the smuggling by force. Brass canoes were fired on by the Customs officials and men were killed. Since the Brassmen's role as middlemen had also been affected, trade with the interior being direct, they were suddenly deprived of their livelihood. Food became desperately short; there were outbreaks of smallpox, and people in the villages came near to starvation. This dangerous position, aggravated by the arrogant acts and behaviour of many Company officials, resulted in strong protests and, when these proved unavailing, in armed revolt.

* *Brass* is a small Nigerian town situated at the mouth of the Brass river. The Brass tribes, or Brassmen, possibly derived their name from the brass utensils and bars which they accepted from the early European traders in exchange for slaves and palm oil.

The crucial date was November 1894, when C. M. Macdonald, who had been appointed H. M. Commissioner and Consul General of the Niger Coast Protectorate three years earlier, declared himself unable to redress the wrongs the Brassmen had suffered. King Koko thereupon vowed that he and his people would die by the sword but never by hunger.

Late in December 1894, Akassa, where the Royal Niger Company had its engineering workshops and trading headquarters, was attacked. A force of over one thousand warriors, well organized and carrying big guns in their canoes, entered the town at four o'clock in the morning, catching its inhabitants completely by surprise. Most of the Company's African employees were slaughtered while they slept, but the Europeans —because of the providential arrival of a British steamer— managed to escape. Koko and his men then sacked Akassa, looting the warehouse and stores with great thoroughness. Returning to Nembe, the Brass capital, they killed a number of their captives, with appropriate ritual, and celebrated their victory by indulging in a jubilant, cannibalistic orgy.

Goldie was astounded at what had happened, and demanded a punitive expedition against the rebels and their total annihilation. The action taken against Nembe fell a great deal short of that, for there was much sympathy in official circles for the Brassmen, who, in any case, put up a stout resitance.

V

Meantime other, and even more serious, dangers were threatening. At about the same time that Akassa was being pillaged a French gunboat steamed into the Niger, and French expeditions intruded into territories which, though claimed by the Company, were ineffectively occupied. Further complications arose when the Colonial Office pressed Goldie to undertake the conquest of Ilorin, in northern Yorubaland, with a view to strengthening the British position there.

At that critical juncture another dominant figure appeared on the Nigerian scene. Frederick John Dealty Lugard, born in Madras in 1858, had served in the Afghan War, in the Sudan campaign for the relief of Gordon, and in the Burma operations, after the fall of King Thebaw, in 1886–7. Later he had been employed by the British East African Company (incorporated by royal charter in 1888) and had distinguished himself by his intervention in Uganda when the Germans imposed a treaty on the Kabaka. Shortly after his arrival in Nigeria, Captain Lugard (as he then was) received instructions from the Royal Niger Company to lead an expedition into Borgu, with the object of making treaties with native rulers, in a region imminently open to French penetration. His efforts were successful, for he managed to forestall an expedition, under Captain H. A. Decoeur, which had similar designs in the disputed area.

These manoeuvrings and skirmishings in Borgu were eventually settled at the conference table in Paris, but not before relations between France and Britain had been strained almost to breaking point. In fact, the Niger crisis of 1897–8 came perilously near to involving the two countries in war; it also marked the beginning of the end for the Royal Niger Company, whose inadequacies, military and financial, were apparent to all.

VI

Criticism of the Company mounted to a new crescendo, but the home Government was understandably reluctant to dispense with the valuable service it was rendering, at little or no cost to the British taxpayer. Goldie, therefore, managed to throw dust in the eyes of the investigators, official and un-official, bent on delving into the Company's affairs, and so, once again, succeeded in extending its lease of life.

In December, 1896, he had begun the military campaign for which Joseph Chamberlain, then Colonial Secretary, had been pressing. The objectives were threefold: to curb the Emir of Ilorin's slave raids into the territories of surrounding states, to induce in him a more favourable attitude towards British interests in mid-Nigeria, and to settle outstanding boundary disputes.

Goldie, placing himself at the head of a diminutive but well-armed force, steamed up the Niger, and prepared for battle; in the first instance against Nupe, which, in his opinion, constituted a more serious danger than Ilorin, because of its greater military strength. To safeguard his rear, and protect Akassa from further attack by the Brassmen, he had persuaded the Government to station troops of the West India regiment in the delta. Even so, the campaign was, as no one realised better than Goldie himself, a gambler's fling. 'We are now risking', he confessed, 'the whole existence of the Company against immense odds.' In regard to manpower he was, indeed, outnumbered by fifty to one.

However, Goldie's men—consisting of five hundred African soldiers and thirty officers—had all the advantages of science on their side, ranging from tinned food to light guns that could be taken apart for ease of transport, from electric arclights to incendiary shells. Goldie had, moreover, planned the campaign in advance down to the last detail, and was confident of victory.

On 3rd January, 1897, he and his army left Lokoja, at the confluence of the Niger and Benue rivers, and a week later were in Kabba, which was placed under the Company's protection. At Egbom, the Niger was crossed and the advance on Bida, the capital of Nupe, began. There, on 26th January, 1897, a fierce and decisive battle was fought against the Nupe warriors, gathered in their thousands round the walls of the city. Dressed in flowing white robes, and for the greater part mounted on horseback, they must have struck at least a momentary chill into the hearts of the attackers. When Goldie approached to within about a mile of the Nupe stronghold a cavalry charge was launched against him, with such devastating effect that his little army was forced to retire.

The Nupe horsemen, and their non-combatant supporters watching from the walls of Bida, raised a great shout of triumph, believing that the fight was over. Goldie's troops, however, formed themselves into a square, and in the face of repeated cavalry charges, fell back in orderly fashion to their base camp, where the artillery was brought into action. The Nupe cavalry, exposed to heavy fire, had to retreat, and an uneasy truce was then observed until nightfall. During the pause, a special long-range gun arrived, which Goldie immediately trained on Bida, scoring a direct hit on the town centre with the first shell. Next day, in the morning, the Royal

Niger Company's troops, again in square formation, began the artillery siege—the main target being the Emir's palace. After a short but intense bombardment, the city was ablaze from end to end and, the Nupe army having scattered, Goldie marched in to take possession. As a result of this action, the whole of Nupe came under the Company's jurisdiction.

There is no need to describe the campaign against Ilorin in detail. Goldie adopted the same tactics as at Bida: advancing in square formation, beating off wild, mass cavalry charges with machine gun fire, and finally shelling the city into surrender. On the afternoon of 16th February, 1897 the Royal Niger Company's flag was flying over the smoking ruins of the citadel, and Emir Suliman, promptly presented with a treaty, had no alternative but to capitulate and sign.

VII

Hardly had the smoke pall over Ilorin cleared than news arrived of the occupation of Bussa and Fort Goldie, higher up the Niger, by a French expeditionary force. Goldie endeavoured to deal with that situation by diplomacy and reasonable discussion. Unfortunately, the French commander, Bretonnet, refused to parley: the Company's rights in the Middle Niger, he declared, were not recognized, and he was under instructions to establish effective occupation of the region on behalf of the French Republic. Goldie's expostulations that France and Britain had long ago agreed the Company's claims to Bussa were dismissed with a polite shrug of the shoulders. The matter evidently was one that only their respective Governments could settle.

Goldie who had gone to Bussa in person—without an armed guard—was disappointed that his attempts at an amicable, on-the-spot agreement should have been turned down so brusquely. Since further discussion was plainly useless, he returned to his headquarters, pausing just long enough, at Asaba, to issue an oddly-timed proclamation to the effect that slavery was abolished throughout the Company's territories.

A clause in the charter had expressly provided that the Company should to the best of its power and, as far as might be possible, abolish by degrees any system of domestic servitude existing among the native inhabitants; and no foreigner, whether European or not, should be allowed to own slaves of any kind in the Company's territories. Until that moment, however, Goldie had done little to implement the clause, and his gesture was probably designed to win sympathy for the Company, to create a new, humanitarian image for it, and placate its liberal critics. Coming after the military victories— which had inspired *The Times* to compare Goldie with Robert Clive and Bida with Plassey—the proclamation was undoubtedly well-calculated to produce agreeable reactions, and to tip the balance of public opinion at home sharply in his favour.

The 'Bussa Affair'—a rehearsal for Fashoda, in the Sudan— precipitated an immediate and dangerous Anglo-French crisis. Not only was the territory of strategic importance but the Company's right to be there, based on treaties of long duration, was indisputable. The British Government, therefore, gave Goldie and the Royal Niger Company its full support. Joseph Chamberlain, the Colonial Secretary, made active preparations for military action, and the issue rapidly took on an international character. Britain, in addition to lodging the most vigorous protests, made its intentions clear beyond doubt by sending gunboats and troops to protect the Company's territories and interests.

Bussa, however, remained firmly in the hands of the French, and since it was apparent that they could only be removed by force, Chamberlain ordered the Governor of Lagos to enrol more men into the constabulary and make plans for the town's recapture. At the same time, preparations to occupy positions in Borgu and Dahomey were put in hand. Lugard was placed in charge of the Frontier Force, which had been considerably strengthened. In August 1897, when the French occupied Kishi and Say, the height of the crisis was reached.

Lugard lost no time in moving into Borgu, where he directly confronted the intruders. Warlike gestures were then made by both sides; there was much hoisting and unfurling of flags, beating of drums, fixing of bayonets, and rattling of sabres. Both sides advanced to the very brink—but the guns remained silent and, in fact, not a single shot was fired.

Neither Britain nor France were ready to wage a costly

war over West Africa and so, in the end, the spirit of compromise prevailed and negotiations began. During the summer of 1898 an Anglo-French Convention managed to hammer out a peaceful settlement of the dispute. France was to withdraw her troops and Britain to retain her political control of the Niger basin. In March 1899 the terms of this agreement were formally ratified.

VIII

Again it was victory. But the course of events had finally demonstrated that the Company was unable, by itself, to defend its extensive territories against predatory Great Powers, or even to keep the native emirs and rulers in a state of permanent subjection. Only the British Government, with its far ampler resources and authority, could do that. No one grasped the realities of the situation better than Goldie, yet he still fought on doggedly to keep the Company in being on its old footing, to achieve at least commercial success and, since the charter appeared in imminent danger, to ensure that the shareholders would be adequately compensated on its revocation. The Government plans for establishing a protectorate gradually crystallized in the summer of 1899, when the Company was relieved of all administrative powers and duties. Though allowed to retain its trading stations, wharves, plant and various other assets, it was required to assign to the Government the benefit of the treaties it had made, its lands and the mineral rights therein. The sum to be paid as compensation was agreed, after hard bargaining, at £865,000, plus half the mineral royalties, which the Government proposed to levy, for a period of ninety-nine years. Goldie and the shareholders, therefore, had every reason to be satisfied.

Towards the end of July, Parliament considered the Bill which authorised expenditure of the public moneys involved. The various opponents of the Company, and in particular the Liverpool traders, then had a glorious opportunity of airing their grievances, dragging its misdeeds into the light of day and objecting to the terms of settlement agreed upon. 'Why', demanded one trenchant critic, 'should a Company, which had broken its charter, established a monopoly right, made large profits, and brought us to the verge of war with France, be so generously treated at the cost of the taxpayer?'

On the whole, however, the debate lacked fire, and there was a strong feeling that the Company, by its empire-building achievement, deserved well of the country. Lord Salisbury went so far as to express his 'high esteem for the adventurers and patriots' to whose efforts the preparation of the West African territory for colonial status was due. When it came to voting, 181 votes were cast for the Bill and 81 against.

A few months later, on 1st January, 1900, an interesting ceremony took place at Lokoja, headquarters of the northern region, in the course of which the Company's flag was hauled down and the Union Jack raised in its place.

IX

Sir George Goldie, 'the Cecil Rhodes of Nigeria,' was proposed as first Governor of the new Crown Colony, but declined the honour. Middle age was beginning to overtake him, though he still had his ambitions and plans for the future. Something made him turn his conquistadorial eye on the Far East and another great river, the Yangste Kiang, flowing through the empire of the crumbling Manchu dynasty. Early in 1900 he actually visited China, to study conditions there at first hand.

The Governorship of the Protectorate of Northern Nigeria, as the new region was called, went to Lugard, who, at forty-one, then entered into the most brilliant phase of his career. He proved to be a capable administrator—one of his outstanding achievements being the introduction of the policy of indirect rule, through the native chieftains. When his term of office expired in 1906, and he went to Hong Kong, the whole of Nigeria had been pacified and effectively brought under British control. Later he returned to Nigeria, and amalgamated the two regions, North and South, into a single administrative unit.

The Royal Niger Company—or rather, the Niger Company Limited, as it became after revocation of the charter—continued its trading activities, on a more or less monopolistic basis, for many more years. The large amount of compensation received enabled it to renew outworn equipment and to extend the scope of its operations. By the early 1920s that position had considerably altered, for two other large trading groups had appeared upon the scene. One was the African and Eastern Trade Corporation, the other Lever Brothers, the rising soap and margarine manufacturers, who used immense quantities of palm oil, and therefore jumped at the offer of a controlling interest in the Niger Company—indeed, entered into a firm commitment without even investigating its affairs. The deal was completed on 1st July, 1920, when the boom that briefly prevailed after the First World War was at its height. That fortunate circumstance enabled the directors of the former Royal Niger Company to demand, and obtain, the golden handshake for its shareholders. Lever Brothers, in fact, paid them £8,000,000 for the business as a going concern. Twelve months later the post-war slump set in; raw-material and commodity prices fell sharply, and but for the fact that the merger was then a *fait accompli* there would undoubtedly have been, so far as the vendors were concerned, a far less happy ending to the story.

* 12 *

Rhodesian Saga

THAT extraordinary combination of scholar, empire-builder, and statesman Cecil Rhodes was born in 1853, into the family of a Bishop's Stortford parson, and went to South Africa as a young man in search of health. Threatened by a serious lung disease, his parents thought that the air of the veldt might affect a cure, and such actually proved to be the case. His elder brother Herbert, a man of adventurous spirit whom Rhodes held in high esteem, was cotton-growing in Natal, and it was natural that the two should join forces. Leaving England on 21st June, 1870, with £2,000 capital loaned to him by an aunt, Cecil arrived at Durban, then no more than a huddle of corrugated iron huts, three months later. A shy and reserved youth of seventeen, whose life expectancy was rated no higher than a few years, he settled down near Pietermaritzburg to the life of a cotton planter.

Thorough in his methods even then, Rhodes made a careful study of the business, and while still in his teens astounded some of the older colonists by achieving something they had considered impossible—making cotton flourish in places where they had predicted it would fail. Besides proving himself a successful agriculturist, Rhodes displayed a great capacity for business and—what was even more surprising—an ability to win the trust and respect of the natives. The cotton-growing phase, however, was destined to be of very short duration.

When the second harvest had been gathered, Cecil set off to join his brother, who had found his way, with many hundreds of other men, to the diamond diggings at Colesberg

155

Kopje, where diamonds in considerable quantity, and some of quite exceptional quality, had been found.

Herbert had pegged a claim, and soon the two brothers were devoting their dynamic energies to this new, and so much more profitable, enterprise. As 'diamond diggers' they were successful from the start, and Rhodes made the fortune that was to provide the basis for all that he attempted in the future. Certainly, without the wealth derived from the Kimberley mines, he would never have achieved the fame he did, nor could the grandiose plans with which his name has become so inseparably associated ever have been embarked upon.

When Herbert left South Africa for a visit to England in 1872, Cecil was left in charge of the various claims they had acquired and though only nineteen years of age, mastered the whole technique of washing, sorting, marketing, controlling labour, and resisting the encroachments of other diggers— many of them men of strong will and reckless character, who were easily provoked to violence.

After the law had been amended to allow diggers to hold more than a single claim, Rhodes adopted the policy of buying out other diggers, which finally resulted in his becoming virtual controller of the Kimberley diamond mines. His investments turned out well, and 'Rhodes' Luck,' which he himself later contended was merely the result of 'getting up early', became proverbial.

Despite the hard work that this feverish bid for riches entailed, the youthful pioneer's energies were by no means exhausted. Already, he had begun to dream of a vast African empire, of territories extending from the Cape to Cairo over which the British flag was to fly. At the same time, he was studying hard, for he had decided, when his means and circumstances permitted, to go to Oxford and take a degree.

II

This ambition Rhodes fulfilled in 1881, at the age of twenty-eight. He graduated as M.A. from Oriel College, and then immediately returned to Kimberley where, in partnership with other men, he joined in the great struggle that was developing for control of the diamond mines. Already in 1880, the De Beers Mining Company had been formed to work the many claims that had been bought up. A part of the De Beers Mine, however, remained in the hands of a rival group. The Kimberley Central Mining Company, dominated by Barney Barnato and Wolf Joel, pursued its own course, and although Rhodes put forward proposals for an amalgamation they were rejected. Many excellent reasons existed for such a merger, the most obvious one being the need to regulate the flow of diamonds into a market that was rapidly becoming saturated.

Eventually Rhodes, by stepping up production and threatening a 'take-over bid', outwitted Barnato and his associates, and the amalgamation of the diamond mines, for which he had striven, was forced through. A single Company, De Beers Consolidated, was incorporated in 1888, with Cecil Rhodes in virtual control. It was a great personal triumph, and a sound move commercially for, from then on, supplies of South African diamonds were related to the demand, and the threatened market collapse was averted.

Even at that stage, it may be remarked, Rhodes's fertile brain had matured the scheme for a South African chartered company, modelled on the East India Company, and authorized to subdue and colonize as great an area of the continent as possible. The amalgamation of the diamond mines was not an end in itself, so far as Rhodes was concerned, but merely a means, a stepping stone, to much greater things.

III

Two years prior to the formation of De Beers, many of the diamond prospectors had trekked into the Transvaal where, on the Witwatersrand, gold had been struck. The curious rock formations in the neighbourhood of what is now Johannesburg had for long excited the curiosity of miners—though not until 1886 was it proved that they contained gold. When it seemed certain that the deposits were on an unprecedented scale, Rhodes lost no time, but with Alfred Beit and other associates, began buying up land. Eventually, the properties were combined and a gold mining corporation came into being—Consolidated Goldfields of South Africa, a company that, like De Beers, was destined to prosper.

The discovery of gold on the Rand resulted in a great influx of British and other miners into the Transvaal, which was occupied by Dutchmen hostile to the British colonists. A vigorous and independent republic, it lay like a barrier across the path to the northern regions on which Rhodes had cast a covetous and imperialistic eye. With the Transvaal and President Kruger in the way, all dreams of expansion to the Zambesi were in vain.

An alternative way, however, was wide open. Looking at the map, Rhodes saw that Bechuanaland was the 'Suez Canal', as he later put it, through which the emigrants must inevitably pass. Against stubborn opposition from the Cape Government, Rhodes appealed to the British Parliament to take over the administration of Bechuanaland; and in 1885 the first steps towards the establishment of a Protectorate were actually taken. At last the road was clear; the trail to Rhodesia could be blazed, and the dream that had filled his imagination ever since he landed at Durban looked as if it might be realized.

But beyond Bechuanaland, in the country that lay between the Transvaal and the Zambesi, were further battles to be fought. The Portuguese had tried to annex the country, which was ruled over by a chief named Lobengula, and the Dutch too had their designs. Nor must the German ambitions in Matabeleland be overlooked. Rhodes, with characteristic audacity, decided to forestall them all, and to bring the territories under British rule. How he did this is a rather long and complicated story.

Briefly, Lobengula was persuaded in 1888 to make a grant to Rhodes of all the mineral rights in the territory. At once a frenzied northward rush of miners and speculators began. Rhodes's promised land, stretching far across to the other side of the Zambesi, had been reached. The home Government approved the action taken, and Rhodes now turned seriously to the task of forming a company, incorporated under a royal charter, to develop Matabeleland and its resources.

IV

The idea was to form a joint stock company, modelled on the Elizabethan pattern, with a monopoly and full authority over the territories it had acquired. Sufficient capital was to be raised to enable the company to undertake the initial exploration, development, and defence. No contribution of any kind was to be called for from the British Exchequer; all that Parliament was asked to do was to set the seal of its approval on the adventure, to give the company official standing by facilitating the grant of a royal charter.

The petition was presented in July, 1889, at a time when Rhodes was in London—lionized by Society, and lauded by the City, as an imperialist of a new and most engaging type. It took several months for those in authority to smooth out the difficulties and placate objectors. Rhodes, fretting with impatience, returned to Kimberley to further his project while awaiting the result.

Everything was decided in October, 1889, when the Queen's charter was granted, incorporating the British South Africa Company, confirming the concession, and delegating powers to its directors—at least until 1905—of a most comprehensive kind.

V

Things now began to move in the desired direction, and Rhodes lived through some of the most strenuous and exciting days of his life. He had obtained his charter for a great joint stock company, whose terms of reference were almost as autocratic as those of the chartered companies of the seventeenth and eighteenth centuries. The lands in the heart of Africa, on which his ambitions had been set, were occupied by the Company's personnel. A railway and a telegraph line were under construction, with the object of linking Mashonaland and Capetown together. Rhodes was now very much in the limelight, and in 1890, when Sir Gordon Sprigg resigned the premiership of Cape Colony, there was little disagreement as to who should take his place.

The implications of this development need hardly be stressed. Rhodes, as managing director of the British South Africa Company, already wielded great economic power, and to this was now added political authority. Both the Dutch and British settlers had a high degree of faith in him at that time, and it looked as if nothing could prevent him from succeeding in the vast enterprise to which he had put his hand.

Criticism there undoubtedly was, but it mainly expressed doubts as to whether one man could combine and perform such a variety of responsible tasks. His critics, presumably, did not realize that Rhodes was deliberately subordinating the secondary interests to the primary one. The goldfields, De Beers, the Chartered Company, were but the instruments through which he hoped to realize his concepts, first, of a union between British and Dutch South Africa, and, second, of a Cape Colony reaching to the Zambesi and beyond. He declared that he could advantageously integrate his functions as prime minister with his company directorships, 'one with the other, and each to the benefit of all'.

The name of Dr F. L. Jameson, Rhodes's life-long friend and medical adviser, now becomes prominent in the complicated Rhodesian saga. Difficulties were being experienced at Fort Salisbury, and poor communications hindered the rapid progress on which Rhodes was intent. He sent Jameson to Mashonaland as representative of the British South Africa Company, to deal with the situation in the way he thought best.

What the doctor had mainly to contend with was the Matabele's fierce resentment of the white man's intrusion into their country. Many of them thought that the old chief, Lobengula, had blundered when granting the concession. This opposition, complicated by differences between the Matabele and Mashona tribesmen, eventually made war against the Matabele inevitable.

The cost of carrying out military operations was borne entirely by the shareholders of the Chartered Company, and by Rhodes personally, with the Colonial Office keeping an eye on events from afar. With almost the whole of the white settlers enrolled into the punitive force, the Matabele 'impi' were engaged in a series of battles, and completely shattered. Lobengula fled, and the flag of the British South Africa Company was hoisted over his deserted kraal. The ceremony took place on the site now occupied by the city of Bulawayo, with a population of fifty thousand.

VI

Rhodes's career, up to this point, had been a triumphal procession, but over-confidence led him, in 1894–5, to make a mistake so serious that it imperilled his reputation as a leader, and might have resulted in dissolution of the company of which he was the animating spirit. Though ever striving to unite Dutch and British interests, Rhodes took sides in the dispute that presently arose between Kruger, redoubtable President of the Transvaal, and the Uitlanders —Britishers who had settled in the Dutch territories and were not only excessively taxed but denied the right to vote. Persuasion having failed to move the President, the Uitlanders planned an uprising in Johannesburg, and Rhodes decided to support them with armed help from outside. Since he was prime minister at the time, the action was indefensible, as he later admitted, and had disastrous consequences. Both he and the British South Africa Company were thrown under a cloud of suspicion that was never wholly dispelled. A successful outcome to the famous 'Jameson Raid' of 1896 might, conceivably, have put a different complexion on the situation—but it turned out a complete fiasco. Dr Jameson and his force of 800 men did, indeed, reach Johannesburg, but the expected revolt of the Uitlanders failed to take place, and the invaders, with their supplies exhausted, were surrounded and forced to surrender.

Rhodes received a sharp reprimand from the British High Commissioner for this unwarranted breaking into the territory of a friendly foreign State in times of peace. He was, moreover, warned that if it should be proved that the British South Africa Company had, in fact, set Jameson in motion, Parliament might think fit to revoke the charter, and force the Company's dissolution. Rhodes resigned his position as prime minister and, for the time being, his political career was at an end.

Fallen from grace, he turned his back on the Cape and, in chastened mood, went to work out a new philosophy in the open spaces of the new lands to the north.

VII

The charter was not, in the event, revoked, and Rhodes's fears in that respect were allayed, but he lost his directorship. Fresh troubles then assailed him, the most serious of which was a native rebellion against the Company and its officials. Then, when the Matabele had been crushed, the shadow of the Boer War fell across Africa, and Rhodes was recalled to political life. At the elections that were held, his 'Progressive Party' polled a majority of the votes, and soon he was back in his old dominating position—reinstated on the board of the British South Africa Company, and spokesman for his party. Again the policy of seeking to unite Dutch and British was pursued. He pressed forward with his railway plans, visited Egypt, and interviewed the German Kaiser, with a view to constructing a transcontinental telegraph line.

Meantime, relations between Dutch and British in South Africa were rapidly deteriorating, the attempts at rapprochement failed, and in 1899 war broke out. Kruger's defeat was encompassed in 1902, the year in which Rhodes died, and seven years later the Union of South Africa, which he had so consistently advocated, was an accomplished fact.

VIII

This tangled story of Cecil Rhodes and the British South Africa Company underlines only too well the extent to which Britain relied, late into the nineteenth century, on commercial adventurers, men who combined the attributes of the conquistador with those of the colonist and trader. Rhodes was, undoubtedly, one of the greatest of them all. Unashamedly an imperialist and empire builder of the old school, he yet had in him a redeeming streak of imagination and creativity, admired even by his bitterest opponents.

Now for a few words about the Chartered Company, the executive arm by which so many of his aims were furthered. Its basis was, of course, the Lobengula Concession of 1888, through which the mineral rights in Matabeleland and Mashonaland were acquired. Without the Company, backed as it was by Parliament, the history of South Africa would assuredly have been very different. Its objects, as outlined in the charter, were to establish British supremacy in the Cape and its hinterland, to develop the wealth of the extensive territories that came to be known as Rhodesia, and to raise the standard of life of the native population. These were three separate and gigantic tasks, too large and responsible for any joint stock organization to undertake without considerable State support.

The extraordinary thing about the British South Africa Company is that it managed to accomplish as much as it did on its own initiative and by its own efforts. Avowedly the means by which Britain hoped to extend her influence over wide areas of the 'dark continent', the Company was yet left to take all the early risks and hazards, to wage the first armed struggles, to bear the costs of the development projects and of military occupation. Not, indeed, until 1924, when Southern Rhodesia became part of the British Empire, was the administrative burden it had borne for thirty-five years, lifted from its shoulders. That these responsibilities, discharged in an admirable way, had been a drain upon its resources is apparent from the fact that prior to 1924 the Company paid no dividend. November of that year saw the first distribution of sixpence per share. A landmark is to be noted in 1933, when the Company sold its mineral rights in South Rhodesia to the South Rhodesian Government, and ceased from that date to have any interest in the accruing royalties.

IX

Six years later, in 1939, the British South Africa Company —'Chartereds' on the Stock Exchange—celebrated its fiftieth birthday. In 1957 its affairs were completely reorganized to qualify it, provisionally, as an overseas trading corporation. Supplemental charters had been granted from time to time—the first in 1900, and the last in 1962—to reflect the changing circumstances and conditions. In September 1961, the Company's principal assets consisted of the mineral rights throughout Northern Rhodesia (until 1968), the mineral rights over 16,000 square miles in Nyasaland, all the shares of the Rhodesia Railway Trust Ltd., and citrus estates in South Africa covering 134,000 acres.

By the time that the seventy-fifth anniversary of the Chartered Company's foundation was reached, in 1964, the world had passed through a second series of wars and revolutions. In Africa, the black men were demanding that their lands—bartered away by Lobengula for a thousand rifles, a steamboat on the Zambesi, and a handful of silver—should be restored to them and white supremacy brought to an end. The winds of change were blowing across the tawny brushlands in hurricane force. Everyone saw that the old forms of European colonialism were on the point of being challenged as never before.

When in October 1964, Northern Rhodesia was transformed into the Republic of Zambia, the interests of the British South Africa Company were, of course, vitally affected. Just prior to the grant of independence, there had been a clash between the North Rhodesian and British Governments over the royalties from the rich Rhodesian copperbelt. The question was whether the Company would, or would not, go on receiving these royalties (which had already netted £170m.) until 1986, when the agreements expired. London took the legalistic view that the Company, whose claim rested on treaties negotiated by Cecil Rhodes, was entitled to a continuation of the copper royalties. Lusaka vigorously challenged the validity of the old treaties and refused to go on paying. In the end a compromise was reached, under which the Company was offered and accepted £4m. as compensation for the surrender of its rights. That major change of fortune, though it posed certain problems for the future, did not, of course, mark the end.

In March 1965, the British South Africa Company merged with two City mining companies to form Charter Consolidated Ltd., of which it is now the wholly-owned subsidiary. It has become part of a powerful group, with massive financial resources, and a wide spread of interests. No doubt there are interesting pages of the saga still to be written: but the period of high drama, of fighting wars, building railways, and generally bearing the white man's burden, is over—which, from a shareholder's point of view, may be no bad thing!

* 13 *

The Falkland Islands Company

JOHN DAVIS, the English navigator and explorer, sailing the stormy South Atlantic in 1592, was probably the first human being ever to set eyes on the group of islands lying some three hundred miles east of the Patagonian coast. Sir Richard Hawkins a year or two later, the Dutchman Sebald de Weert in 1600, and various other navigators noted their existence without troubling to give them more than a cursory inspection. It was in 1690 that another English navigator, Captain Strong of the *Welfare*, applied to them the name 'Falkland Islands'— in honour of Viscount Falkland, loyal supporter of King Charles I during the Civil War and liberal patron of men-of-letters and scholars.

As a glance at the map will show, the group consists of two main islands, West Falkland and East Falkland, and some two hundred islets. Their total area is less than 5,000 square miles, and even today they support a population far less than that of many a thriving English village. The Falklands have been referred to as the 'British Empire's Sub-Arctic Outpost', yet they enjoy a climate, temperate and subject to no violent extremes, very much the same as ours. The scenery, reminiscent of parts of Scotland and of the Orkneys, is wild and rugged. There are hills—Mount Osborne, believed to be the highest, rises to 2,312 feet—and stretches of bleak moorland, broken by irregular outcrops of quartz rock. Strong winds blow over the islands throughout much of the year and, as a result, there are few cultivated areas or trees. How then does this pocket-sized Crown Colony, which leaps into the newspaper headlines periodically when Argentina revives an old and dubious claim, earn its living?

The answer is to be found in its sheep farms, its population of approximately 635,000 sheep, of which 280,000 are owned by the Falkland Islands Company, and its annual wool clip.

II

After Strong's landing, the first of which there is any record, the Falklands began to attract the attention of other European nations. In 1764 the French, who called them the *Îles Malouines*, established the settlement of Port Louis on East Falkland's north-east coast. Two years later the islands were ceded to Spain, though in the meantime Britain had sent Commodore John Byron to take possession of them and establish the first British garrison. In 1774 it was evacuated for reasons of economy, but the Spaniards remained until 1806 when they, too, decided that the *Islas Malvinas* were hardly worth troubling about.

Fourteen years later the Republic of Argentine made its first claim to the islands, and in 1829 appointed a Governor, Louis Vernet, to take charge of them on its behalf. He made the mistake, two years later, of arresting three United States ships for alleged breaches of the seal-fishing regulations. This action was regarded by the U.S. authorities, who held the Falklands to be *terra nullius* or 'nomansland', as tantamount to piracy. The corvette *Lexington* was, therefore, ordered to make for the islands and deal with the situation. Her commander demolished the Argentinian settlement and in December, 1831, declared the islands to be 'free of all governance'. Argentina, in the following year, defiantly appointed a new Governor, but a mutiny broke out and he was killed. Next, in 1832, followed a move by Britain, which had never relinquished and now decided to reassert her sovereignty over the islands. H.M.S. *Clio*, under the command of Captain Onslow, arrived at Port Louis on 2nd January, 1833, and ordered the Argentinian garrison to surrender and leave, which it did within three days. The British flag was then hoisted, and a few years later the first civil administration was authorized and set up. Despite protests from Argentine, the United States declined to regard the British occupation as a violation of the Monroe doctrine, and took no action.

The story of the Falkland Islands Company, which had been nicknamed the 'Admirable Crichton' of Companies, because of its versatility, begins at about this stage. Samuel Fisher Lafone and his brother Alexander Ross Lafone, engaged in the cattle trade at Montevideo, made enquires about the south of East Falkland Island and acquired the absolute right to subdue and slaughter the wild cattle there. The animals—'fat, magnificent, and better than those of the Plate'—were the descendants of a herd introduced by the French in 1764, and had increased in numbers to an estimated total of 40,000. When, some years later, the Lafones ran into financial difficulties they suggested to their principal creditors—Ricketts, Boutcher & Co., a firm of London merchants—that a joint stock company should be formed to take over their interests in the islands.

III

A preliminary prospectus was issued in which the existing assets were enumerated—land, buildings, plant and cattle to an estimated value of £212,000—and the objects briefly stated as those of a trading company, with colonization as an 'adjunctive benefit'. Later, on 24th April, 1851, a preliminary meeting of the Falkland Islands Company was held and its aims were then more fully defined, i.e. to set up an establishment of *gauchos* for the taming of wild cattle; to increase the supply and stock of sheep on East Island; to establish a general store; to provide regular postal communications between the islands and the mainland, as well as with Europe—an advantage which the Colony had not previously enjoyed.

The actual incorporation of the Company was effected in 1851, and the royal charter was granted in the following year. On the modest starting capital of £100,000 it was estimated, far too optimistically, that an annual profit of £20,000 would be made, or even more, for the islands were being considered by the Government for a convict settlement, and additional revenues were expected from the whale and seal fisheries, and from peat.

In fact, the first few years of the Falkland Islands Company proved to be difficult. Nothing quite came up to expectations.

The cattle killings yielded disappointing results, and heavy losses were incurred on the mail contract. By April, 1853, the Company was in such financial straits that the directors were tempted to wind up. Better counsels, however, prevailed, and despite many discouraging factors they carried on until, ten years later, the tide slowly began to turn.

The sheep were beginning to prove profitable, and considerable areas of freehold land were therefore purchased. The shares, which had fallen far below their nominal value, then began to rise, and by 1902, when the Company was registered under the Companies Act, a dividend of $12\frac{1}{2}$ per cent was paid. Subsequently, the capital was increased to £350,000 and farms at Port Louis and Fitzroy, and property at Stanley, were purchased. By 1940 the Company was farming over a million acres.

Much of the solid progress achieved by the Falkland Islands Company from 1867 onwards, when the initial difficulties had been surmounted, was due to the energy, wisdom, and persistence of its Colonial Manager, F. E. Cobb, who lived and worked in the islands for twenty-three years. Eventually, on his return to England, he was appointed managing director, and served in that capacity for another thirty-one years. Even after his retirement in 1922 he maintained a lively interest in the Company and its affairs.

IV

Shrewd and observant, Cobb had noted on his arrival in Stanley as a young man that the wool of the Falkland Islands sheep was the 'loosest, coarsest, and most hairy' anywhere to be found. He drew the conclusion that there had been mismanagement at some time in the past and, with a view to rectifying matters, appointed an experienced New Zealand sheep farmer to take charge of the Company's flocks. The result soon became apparent in wool of greatly improved quality.

For many years the Cheviot strain had predominated on the islands, though others—Southdowns, Romneys, and Lincolns had been tried. In 1920 the Company went to Tierra del Fuego and purchased several hundred rams of a breed renowned for the fineness of its wool, and the experiment proved a great success. The crossbred wool, in fact, found such favour in London, the world's most exacting and competitive market, that it was able to command the top price then prevailing—22d. per pound.

After 1870 Cobb took over management of the farm at Darwin—so-named after the great scientist Charles Darwin, who visited Port Louis with Captain Fitzroy in H.M.S. *Beagle* in 1834—and, despite the fact that as Colonial Manager he had many other duties to perform, firmly set the Company on a footing of prosperity. When, in 1891, he relinquished his appointment in the Colony, the number of sheep had increased fourfold.

Thirty years later, when Cobb was in London, it was decided that Darwin was no longer suitable as a site for a modern sheep station. The wool sheds there were badly placed, the paddocks inadequate, and the harbour unsuitable. A move was, therefore, made to Goose Green, where ample space was available, and new farm buildings, paddocks, a wool shed and dip were constructed, close to a disused canning factory. Among other things, this move necessitated the building of a suspension bridge across Bodie Creek, so that the sheep could easily be driven to Goose Green, there to be shorn under the expert eyes of the manager and a Bradford wool-classer.

V

Like the Argonauts of old, the Falkland Islands Company had gone in search of the Golden Fleece, and had like them succeeded in its quest. Sheep farming became, and still remains, the basic activity—the chief revenue earner and dividend producer. From the very beginning, however, the Company had made a point of diversifying its activities. The establishment of a general store and the provision of a regular postal service with the outside world, had been among the Company's original objects. In regard to the mail service, a schooner—the *Amelia*—had been purchased in 1852, and had actually reduced the cost of sending a letter to England by more than half. Nevertheless, the mail contract proved to be a liability rather than an asset, and so, with Govermnent permission, it was abandoned only two years after the start. Eventually, in the 1930s, a fresh mail contract, on more advantageous terms, was negotiated.

The store, too, had been founded in the early pioneering days—at Stanley, the future capital—and the Company later acquired the store of a go-ahead competitor, J. M. Dean, together with a hotel, a tavern, and several houses. Presently as the population of the islands grew, and their economy developed, it became necessary for the Company to provide banking facilities. On the farms it assumed responsibility for the settlers' educational, medical and religious needs. The first steam engine and the first telephone system in the islands were installed at the Company's initiative. From J. M. Dean it took over, in addition to the flourishing store, several hulks for storage purposes and a fleet of ships. At Stanley, a recognized port of refuge for vessels that had taken a battering while rounding Cape Horn, a busy ship-repairing business was developing. These ancillary activities of banking and storekeeping, though not ship-repairing, are maintained to the present day.

Among the many important agencies held by the Company are those of the Admiralty, Lloyd's, and the Royal Insurance Company; it was, until recently, an accredited correspondent of Reuter's, the international news agency.

VI

Dr Johnson, in the eighteenth century, described the Falkland Islands as 'thrown aside from human use, stormy in winter, barren in summer, islands which not even the southern savages have dignified with habitation'. He had, of course, no first-hand knowledge of the weather, which has been much maligned, but undoubtedly he was right in saying that primitive man appears to have avoided them, for evidence of human life, prior to the arrival of civilized Europeans, had yet to be discovered. Even John Davis and the early navigators who followed him were not tempted to make landings. However, as we have already noted, quite a scramble for the Falkland Islands developed later—Spain, France, and Britain being the principal contenders.

The French and Spanish claims were eventually dropped, and Britain, after 1833, was left in undisputed possession— undisputed, that is to say, by anyone except the Argentinians, whose garrison at Port Louis had been evicted by Captain Onslow, of H.M.S. *Clio*. Argentina's claim, based on her brief occupation of the islands and their proximity to the South American mainland, was more persistent, and in recent years has given rise to at least one bizarre incident. Late in September, 1966 a group of twenty Argentine nationalists, one of them a girl, 'hi-jacked' an air liner at gunpoint and forced the pilot to land on Stanley racecourse. There followed a melodramatic attempt to seize the islands on behalf of the Argentine, but the President, General Ongania, disavowed the rebels and promised that they would be punished for their piratical actions. A few days later, they were talked into surrender by a Roman Catholic priest.

The incident, reported under banner headlines in the London newspapers, was apparently started as a high-spirited prank—possibly touched off by the Argentine disappointment at having lost the World Association Football Cup to Britain just previously—but assumed more serious aspects when the exuberant Latins, hailed as heroes in Buenos Aires, threatened to start guerilla warfare in the islands. A British frigate, stationed at Simonstown in South Africa, thereupon received her sailing orders.

The attempt to seize the Falkland Islands failed but the official Argentinian attitude has ever since continued to be challenging and obdurate. Britain, however, has repeatedly declared her intention of standing firm and upholding her sovereign rights in the islands.

VII

Half a century earlier, of course, the Colony and the Company had faced a far greater danger. Shortly after the First World War had broken out, a German naval squadron, under the command of Admiral von Spee, which had defeated a technically inferior British squadron close to the Chilean port of Coronel, appeared suddenly off the Falkland Islands, apparently unaware that a number of British warships—including the *Invincible*, *Inflexible*, and *Carnarvon*—were already there. In the ensuing 'Battle of the Falkland Islands' the entire German squadron was destroyed. Years later a monument was erected in Stanley (by F. E. Cobb) to commemorate the victory, which saved the Colony from falling into German hands.

The islanders, and the officials of the chartered company, heaved a sigh of relief at the narrow escape and went on with their sheep breeding. After the First World War wool prices, in common with those of other commodities, fell sharply, and in succeeding decades fluctuated widely, yet the shareholders received a dividend from 1862 onwards in every year except one. In 1951 the centenary was quietly celebrated.

Two other landmarks in the history of the Falkland Islands Company deserve mention: first, its registration under the Companies Act of 1902 which made it limited as well as chartered, and, secondly, the decision of the directors in 1962 to seek a Stock Exchange quotation for its shares, the dealings in which had increased considerably. Buyers and sellers had until then been brought together by the Company itself or on the Stock Exchange unofficially. After the quotation had been obtained they could transact business in the normal way— through a stockbroker. The authorized capital at the beginning of 1968 was £1,500,000, of which £930,000 had been issued.

The Falkland Islands Company, whose London offices are in Pall Mall, is the oldest, indeed the sole survivor, of the several overseas trading companies incorporated by royal charter in the heyday of the Victorian era. That, of course, is only another way of saying that it has been the one unqualified and enduring success.

* 14 *

The British North Borneo Company

BORNEO, the third largest island in the world—forest-clad, mountainous, and picturesque—has interested the white man ever since it was discovered by Portuguese voyagers in the sixteenth century. The name is a variant of Brunei, a small state on the north-west coast, formerly under the absolute rule of a native sultan. One of the first Englishmen to be impressed by Borneo's great natural beauty and economic potentialities was James Brooke, who wrote an extraordinary, indeed unique, chapter into British colonial history.

Born at Coombe Grove, near Bath, in 1803, Brooke entered the service of the East India Company's army at the age of sixteen. While in Burma, he was badly wounded and soon afterwards invalided home on a small pension. He returned to India in 1830, but was shipwrecked and, his contract with the East India Company lapsing just then, he was left free to determine his future in any way he liked.

Still a young man, and in no hurry to settle down, James Brooke set off on a voyage to China, and in the course of his wanderings saw many of the Indonesian islands. He became obsessed with the idea that he would like to own one of them and bring to its people, still living under primitive conditions, some of the benefits of western civilization.

The opportunity of realizing his dream came in 1835, when his father died, leaving him a fortune of £30,000, part of which he used to equip a small schooner. He set sail in the *Royalist*, of 140 tons burden, in October 1838, and arrived at Kuching, in Sarawak, in the following year. The wildness of the country, its equable climate, and scenic grandeurs were irresistible, and he decided to travel no farther. Soon he had built himself a small wooden bungalow, which became his home and headquarters.

Two years after establishing himself in Borneo, a native rebellion broke out. By taking an active part in suppressing it and restoring law and order, James Brooke earned the gratitude of the Sultan of Brunei, who made him the first 'White Rajah' of Sarawak, with full authority to embark on the civilizing mission on which he had set his heart. He began by waging a vigorous war against the pirates who then infested the South China Sea, and quickly brought about a substantial reduction in the scale of their depredations.

When he died in 1868, Sir James—for he had been knighted twenty years earlier—was succeeded by his nephew, Sir Charles Johnson Vyner Brooke, who ruled as Rajah until 1946, when Sarawak became a British Crown colony.

II

The first white man to acquire an interest in the Bornean territory lying to the north of Sarawak, the American Claude Lee Moses, was another lone adventurer fascinated by the Pacific and its innumerable islands. Chance brought him in 1865 to Labuan where, on approaching the Sultan of Brunei, he managed to secure an important grant of territory. Ten years later, the Austrian Consul-General at Hong Kong, Baron von Overbeck, purchased the concession from Moses, and successfully petitioned the sultan for an extension of the period during which it was to remain valid.

Overbeck had hoped to interest either the Austrian or German Governments in North Borneo, but failing to do so contacted the head of a prosperous firm of English merchants, Dent Brothers and Co., with whom he had done business in the past. The two Dents—Alfred and Edward—were favourably impressed, and sent the baron back to Borneo, where he persuaded the Sultan of Brunei to make further territorial grants. That was the point at which the formation of a joint stock company, to exploit the concessions, was first considered.

North Borneo, roughly pyramidal in form, was at about that time beginning to acquire strategic significance. Its west coast bordered the sea route linking European countries with China and Japan, while the east coast flanked the route between Japan, China and Australia. Moreover, along both coasts were natural harbours and bays in which ocean-going vessels of all sizes could find anchorage and shelter.

The Foreign Office, headed by Lord Salisbury, was, therefore, more than a little interested to learn of the developments that were taking place. As it happened, Alfred Dent was on friendly terms with Sir Julian Paunceforth, permanent under-secretary of the Foreign Office, who suggested that the venture was of sufficient importance to justify incorporation of the Company by royal charter. This, he thought, would give it the quasi-official standing and prestige that it deserved.

Unfortunately, the granting of charters to joint stock companies had been out of fashion since at least 1858 when, as related in an earlier chapter, the East India Company had been forced to surrender its privileges. Mercantile corporations, it was held in the 1870s, should confine themselves to trade and not be allowed to exercise sovereign rights over foreign territories. Certainly, experience had shown that they were very liable to become embroiled in wars and revolts, from the consequences of which they might have to be rescued by Government intervention. There was also the certainty that any such corporation, if granted monopoly rights, would arouse the opposition of rival traders.

Despite the adverse omens, Alfred Dent, who had already sunk £10,000 in the North Borneo project, decided to make formal application for the grant of a charter. Because of certain difficulties created by Spain—which advanced a claim to North Borneo, based on the conquest of Sulu—the Government was unable to give an immediate decision. The Dutch, who were in possession of the southern part of the island, also raised objections, and so the matter dragged on inconclusively for several years. Eventually, however, when both the Spanish and Dutch claims failed, the Dent Brothers' application entered the sphere of practical politics.

III

The decisive moves were made in 1881, when the British North Borneo Provisional Association was formed, and Mr Gladstone approved the granting of a royal charter. Six months later, in May 1882, the British North Borneo Company, with a nominal capital of £2,000,000, was formally incorporated.

The charter provided, among other things, that the Company would always remain British in character; that it would prohibit the transfer, wholly or in part, of the benefit of its grants and concessions without permission of the Secretary of State; and that it would not seek any general monopoly of trade. One of the more important clauses invested the Secretary of State with powers of supervision over the Company's proceedings, including the appointment of its principal representative in North Borneo. Other clauses imposed on the Company the obligation to abolish slavery in its territories, to administer justice with due regard to native custom and laws, and to tolerate, without interference, the religion of the natives.

Inevitably, the Government's action stimulated controversy. Already in March, 1881, the setting up of the British North Borneo Company had led to animated discussion in the House of Commons, during the course of which the prime minister—a little on the defensive—had explained that no question of annexation of the territory by Great Britain was involved, and that the Queen's charter, while imposing duties and restraints, conferred no special rights. 'There is not a single privilege,' he declared, 'given to the Company . . . over and above what it has already acquired by title.'

Parliament was satisfied, and the one obdurate critic, strangely enough, was Sir Charles Brooke, the second white rajah of Sarawak, who maintained that the handing over of North Borneo to a group of London mercantile adventurers could only lead to disaster. He had, in fact, his own ambitions in regard to the territory, and remained hostile to the Company throughout the early stages of its career. In the event, this was to extend over a period of sixty years.

IV

Inevitably, the first decade was difficult—full of pioneering hardships and setbacks. The territory had to be thoroughly explored—almost nothing was known about the interior—clearings had to be made in the forests, and administrative centres established at various points. Hardest of all, perhaps, was the task of making contact with the Bornean population, which was not numerous but included Malay and Chinese elements, and gaining its confidence. The Company's officials had to learn the native languages, to familiarize themselves with the local customs and with the diverse modes of living of a polyglot people. They had, above all, to wage an unending war against malaria, smallpox, cholera and other tropical diseases.

Alfred Dent, convinced of the potential wealth of North Borneo, was undoubtedly the driving force behind the developments that took place in those early years. In fact, he filled the role of managing director with admirable competence, formulating both financial and administrative policies. Among his most able supporters was William Hodd Treacher, a young and enthusiastic administrator, who was appointed first Governor of North Borneo, and acted in that capacity throughout the critical period when it was emerging from conditions of near anarchy. The Company's first chairman was Sir Rutherford Alcock, a retired civil servant, whose intimate knowledge of the Far East and Foreign Office contacts were to prove invaluable.

One of the first landmarks in the North Borneo Company's history was the outbreak, in 1884, of a minor revolt. This arose out of the refusal of a local chieftain to allow access to the Godmanton caves, which were used by myriads of swifts as nesting places. The nests had value because they were edible and in great demand among the Chinese, who regarded them as delicacies. The obstructive chieftain demanded an exorbitant toll for use of the path leading to the caves, and, when his authority was questioned, put up a show of force. In an exchange of shots with a small detachment of Company police he was killed. After that there was no further trouble over the birds' nests, which continued to be collected and eventually became an important item of export. A more serious rebellion, led by Mat (Mohammed) Salleh, will be mentioned later.

Another landmark is to be noted in 1888, when the British Government declared North Borneo to be a British Protectorate, a move which greatly strengthened the Company's position and, by underwriting their interests, pleased the shareholders. The terms of the Protectorate were formally signed on 12th May, 1888, by the Marquess of Salisbury on behalf of the Government, and by Sir Rutherford Alcock on the Company's behalf. Thus did the 'State of North Borneo', henceforth the official designation of the territory, come into being.

The knighthood conferred on Alfred Dent in the same year was an indication of the Government's approval of what he and his colleagues had accomplished so far. Even more solid evidence of official confidence came in 1890, when Labuan, the island-colony in the Bay of Brunei, was placed under the Company's jurisdiction.

V

Mention must now be made of another remarkable man whose name is inseparably connected with the development of North Borneo—William Clarke Cowie, a Scotsman who, in 1872, obtained from the Sultan of Sulu permission to establish a trading base at Sandakan Bay on the east coast. He was, at the time, manager of a small Singapore firm, the Labuan Trading Company, and engaged in activities of a somewhat dubious nature. Spain was trying, as she had done before, to assert her authority over the Sulu Archipelago, a chain of islands extending from north-eastern Borneo to the Philippines, which were already under her control. Jolo, the principal island in the Archipelago, was being blockaded by Spanish warships, with a view to depriving the Sulus of outside assistance. Cowie, with a few small ships at his disposal, made capital out of the situation by organizing the supply of arms, ammunition, and other contraband material to the islanders. He was acting, in plain words, as a gun-runner.

Like Brooke of Sarawak, Cowie had opposed the formation

of the British North Borneo Company, and remained un-friendly to it after the charter had been granted. Eventually, when North Borneo was declared a British Protectorate, he returned to London and, admitting that he was unable to defeat the Company, joined it, and created such an impression that within a few years the court elected him to replace Sir Alfred Dent as managing director.

A man of stubborn determination, and from then onward the Company's moving spirit, Cowie embarked on policies that, from time to time, stimulated the keenest controversy. It was considered, for example, that he was precipitate in his plans to construct a trans-Bornean railway, a trunk road and a telegraph line across what was unknown mountain and jungle territory. Certainly he underestimated the difficulties, and the heavy expenditure, that those undertakings would involve.

He was also proved wrong in his assumption that a large native population existed in the interior, and that the persistent labour shortage which had hindered agricultural and trading development would be solved by its discovery. To pay for his ambitious projects and mistakes, both customs dues and taxes had to be increased. An entirely new tax on rice resulted in a virtual cessation of the flow of Chinese immigrants and in an economic stagnation that was to last for ten years. Notwith-standing these and other errors of judgement, Cowie continued to enjoy the unswerving loyalty of the Court of directors and of the shareholders.

It was just after he had taken Dent's place that the first rumblings of the Mat Salleh rebellion were heard. Late in 1894 Salleh, headman of a small community on the Sugut river, was held responsible for the murder of two Dyak traders who had penetrated into his region. The incident was dealt with in a rather clumsy way and rapidly escalated. In July, 1896, Mat Salleh—a man of proud, independent and warlike spirit—was declared an outlaw and hunted down by the police force.

He managed to evade capture and in July, 1897, launched an attack on Gaya, the west-coast island settlement, which he looted and set on fire. The Company made reprisals in kind. Rebel villages and rice crops were destroyed, and Mat Salleh was driven back into the remote interior. There, at Ranau, he built a massive fort and, abandoning the guerrilla tactics he had followed up to that point, withdrew behind its walls, which were in places nine feet thick. This gave him a sense of false security and proved a mistake, for Ranau was at once besieged and, after a brief resistance, overrun.

Cowie, who visited North Borneo early in 1898, tried to persuade Mat Salleh to surrender, promising that if he laid down his arms he and his followers would receive free pardons, and be offered land on which to settle. For one reason and another, the negotiations broke down, and the Company ordered a resumption of hostilities. Cowie, accused of trying to appease a dangerous criminal, whose raids and depredations were alarming the whole territory, lost the confidence of his co-directors for the time being and was divested of all authority.

Mat Salleh, meantime, had gained the support of numerous Bajau and Tegaas tribesmen, and built himself a complex of four new fortresses. The final trial of strength came early in 1900, when the Company was able to mount a major offensive against the rebels. Marching into the interior, the expeditionary force first captured a number of strategic outposts and villages, and then attacked the forts. When, on a dramatic February day, Mat Salleh was killed by a stray shot from a mountain gun, resistance abruptly ceased and the revolt was over.

VI

Just prior to this, the British North Borneo Company had, from its offices at 15 Leadenhall Street, London, published a brief survey of the Colony, compiled from official records, with trade returns and an account of the progress of the chartered company to date. The Government stations, it appears from this informative record, were at that time Labuan, Mempakol, Sugut, Sandakan (the capital), Lahad Datu (Darvel Bay), and Tawao (Cowie Harbour)—all situated on the coast. In the interior were Penungah, Kaningow, Tenom, Beaufort, Bukau and some smaller stations. The entire population of the Company's territory was estimated to be 200,000, three quarters of it living on the west coast.

The list of trading products included birds'-nests, coal, camphor, coconuts, copra, coffee, cotton, fish, gold, gutta percha, india rubber, iron ore, ivory, opium, pearls, pepper, rattans, rice, sago, sharks' fins, shells, sugar, tapioca, tobacco and tortoiseshell. 'Virgin forests', the report added, 'afford an unlimited supply of the best woods for every purpose.'

Timber, indeed, was one of the mainstays of the Bornean economy throughout the period of Company rule. The first shipments of a soft wood resembling cedar had gone to Australia as far back as 1885 and, later, China bought great quantities of cut logs for the making of railway sleepers. Hardwoods, too, proved to be readily saleable.

Tobacco, in the 1890s, was another important item of export. Its cultivation had begun, on a small scale, at Silam on the east coast, at a time when sugar was not paying. When a few bales of this tobacco, produced as an experiment on a single estate, were sent to London in 1884 the leaf was declared to be of excellent quality—and particularly suited for the making of cigars. Within a few years of that initial success, over fifty estates in North Borneo were growing tobacco, and the Government was able to augment its revenue by levying a modest export tax. Not until 1902, when cigarettes began to be smoked in preference to cigars, did this valuable trade decline. By 1930 it had almost ceased.

VII

The first rubber plants reached Borneo in 1882, and within a decade rubber was being commercially grown on the west coast, where conditions were most favourable. When the American and British motor-car industry started to expand, early in the present century, the demand for rubber suddenly boomed and Borneo, in common with Malaya and some other countries of south-east Asia, immediately stepped up production. Easily grown, rubber proved to be more rewarding, in the long run, than either timber or tobacco. Many of the estates were sited by the side of the railway line between two newly-constructed towns, Jesselton and Beaufort, on the

west coast. To encourage the establishment of more plantations, the Company announced in 1905 that rubber would be
free of export tax for the next fifty years. This offer had the
desired stimulating effect: more capital and men were forthcoming, and production increased rapidly. In 1920, before
demand suddenly slumped, North Borneo was exporting ten
million tons of rubber a year.

Gold, which it was believed must exist in considerable
quantities in the mountains and river beds of the territory,
proved a snare and a delusion, despite the most assiduous
prospecting. Nor did seekers after diamonds and oil—which
had been struck in Brunei, Sarawak and Dutch Borneo—
fare any better.

VIII

Here, perhaps, is the right place to emphasize that the British
North Borneo Company was a purely administrative body. It
governed and created the conditions in which commerce
could flourish, but did not itself trade. In that respect, of
course, it differed from most other chartered companies,
such as the East India, Hudson's Bay and Royal Niger Companies which, at least during the early phases of their careers,
combined the two functions. However, by 1899 several sub-
sideries were in operation, including a steamship company,
tobacco companies, a coffee company and a gold syndicate.
These offshoots, which had a combined capital of over
£1,000,000, contributed what they could to the parent
company's profits, which were seldom very large.

The actual government of North Borneo was, from the
outset, firmly vested in the London court of directors, subject
only to the terms and conditions of the royal charter. In
practice, the territory was administered by the Governor,
supported by a colonial secretary, three residents of districts,
and a number of assistant residents. Treasury, Judicial, Public
Works, Harbour, Medical, Land Survey, and Constabulary
Departments attended to financial matters, adjudicated in
legal disputes, studied health problems as they affected the
native population and staff, prospected and developed the

territory, prosecuted criminals, and in general did all those things expected of a civil service.

Cowie, in making his annual report to the shareholders in 1899, stated that the Indian penal code had been adopted almost in its entirety, and that the Government looked to native chiefs and headmen to maintain order within their districts. The rights and customs of the natives, he claimed, were fully respected, and slavery was rapidly dying out. After mentioning that the authorized capital of the Company was then £2,000,000, he briefly reviewed the Company's liabilities and assets, and, aware that dividends had been small and infrequent, hinted at a brighter future.

'On the one side of our balance sheet,' he told the shareholders (whose full confidence he had regained), 'we have £568,000, which represents the Company's paid-up (as distinct from authorized) capital. On the other we have a country as large as Ireland, full of untold natural wealth, plus twenty-five miles of railway [the first train in North Borneo had run in February 1898], three hundred miles of telegraph, a cruiser, jetties, wharves, Government buildings, and all the machinery necessary for control of the native population, including the collection of revenue, which is now increasing annually. We owe nothing.'

He gave the estimated surplus of income over expenditure for the year ending 31st December, 1898 as £16,000—a modest 2½ per cent on the subscribed capital.

IX

The opening decade of the twentieth century was comparatively uneventful. Tobacco gave way to rubber; Cowie was replaced as chairman of the Company by Sir West Ridgeway; an Education Department was formed and an inspector of schools appointed; the boundary with Dutch Borneo was finally settled; a Village Settlement proclamation confirmed the principle of indirect rule to which the Company was committed; native courts were set up in every district; Britain resumed direct responsibility for the administration of Labuan, for reasons of imperial policy. Medical research continued and, among other successes, the remedy for beri beri was discovered as a result of an experiment in Sandakan prison, where the prisoners were fed on a diet of unpolished rice, rich in vitamin B1, instead of the more popular white rice. Cutch, the khaki dye used for military uniforms, began to assume increasing importance on the export list.

The First World War, which broke out in August, 1914, did not directly affect North Borneo, but inevitably resulted in a disruption of trade. A good deal of inconvenience was caused by the withdrawal of German shipping, which had enjoyed a virtual monopoly, from the South Pacific routes. Shortages of rice and other foodstuffs were experienced. Many of the staff, in London as in North Borneo, were either called up or volunteered for military service, with the result that many worth-while development projects had to be shelved. In 1915 a rebellion of the Murut tribes, the most backward in Borneo, who resented the curbs placed on their barbarous custom of head hunting, had to be quelled. Financial difficulties caused by the war then arose: the Company was obliged to borrow money and ran heavily into debt. Nor was its position made any easier when, just after the war, North Borneo's plantations were devastated by a plague of locusts.

Conditions, however, gradually returned to normal, and by 1929 the Company was able to report further substantial progress. Rubber had by then become the principal article of export. At Sandakan and Jesselton, power houses for the generation of electricity had been built. Twelve telephone exchanges were operating in the State (that at Sandakan being fully automatic), and a central bank had been established. Two years later, in 1931, when the Company was celebrating its jubilee, the world economic depression cast its shadow over the territory. Heavy financial losses were incurred and for six years no dividends could be paid.

X

By 1938 the chartered company, despite its excellent performance as an administrative body, had become something of an anachronism, yet, because it relieved the British Government

of all responsibility in regard to North Borneo, it was allowed
to function for another three years. The directors themselves
had for some time been urging the Colonial Office to exercise a
greater measure of control; and in fact a take-over—involving
an outright purchase of the Company's assets—had actually
been considered. No action was taken, however, and the status
quo remained undisturbed even after September, 1939, when
the Second World War broke out.

North Borneo, which had by then attained a favourable
balance of trade and real prosperity, was one of the several
far-eastern countries vulnerable to Japanese attack. The
moment of truth was reached in 1941, when after the raid on
Pearl Harbour, which crippled the U.S. Pacific fleet, and the
sinking of the two British battleships *Prince of Wales* and
Repulse, Japan gained at least a temporary advantage. Like
Malaya, Thailand, Hong Kong and Singapore, Borneo—
Dutch as well as British—was quickly overrun. An army of
25,000 men, supported by warships, carriers and aircraft,
took possession of the towns, villages and estates. The Company,
whose only force consisted of a small native Constabulary with
European officers, was in no position to resist. Promptly, on
arrival of the invaders, its properties were commandeered for
military purposes, and its officials arrested and interned.

The war, in fact, marked the end of the Company's rule.
In June, 1945 the territory was liberated, but new and more
direct means of governing it had obviously to be found. North
Borneo, after four years of Japanese occupation, was wrecked
and exhausted. Great material damage had been done, and to
make this good prior to starting all over again, was clearly
a task beyond the Company's inadequate and overstrained
resources. The question of Sarawak, in similar difficulties,
arose at the same time, and the Government, after due consideration, decided that the only practical course was to take
over both territories.

Under the terms of an agreement dated 1st July, 1946, the
British North Borneo Company received certain advance
payments by way of compensation for its rights and assets. Two
weeks later, on 15th July, when North Borneo became a
Crown Colony, the officials in London paid off its last debts,

heaped its accumulated records into tin boxes, and issued the obituary notices. The Company, with an exemplary record extending over sixty years, ceased to exist.

With it went the whole concept, so hopefully revived by the Victorians, of the chartered corporation as a means of building empire, administering colonies, and developing overseas trade.

Select Bibliography

The Principal Navigations, Voyages, and Discoveries of the English Nation. Richard Hakluyt. First published in 1589 and later edited and enlarged.

The Constitution and Finance of English, Scottish and Irish Joint Stock Companies to 1720. William Robert Scott.

The Economic History of England. Ephraim Lipson (1959–61).

The Early History of the Russia Company, 1553–1603. Thomas Stuart Willan (1953).

The Treatise of Commerce. John Wheeler, secretary and historian of the Merchant Adventurers of England (1601).

The Merchant Adventurers of England, their Laws and Ordinances. W. E. Lengelbach (1902).

The East India Company in eighteenth-century politics. L. S. Sutherland (1952).

Traders' Dream: the Romance of the East India Company. R. H. Mottram (1939).

East India House. Sir William Foster (1924).

The Hudson's Bay Company as an imperial factor, 1821–1869. John S. Galbraith (1957).

The Governor and Company of Adventurers of England Trading into Hudson's Bay during Two Hundred and Fifty years, 1670–1920. Sir William Schooling. (Published by the Company in 1920.)

The Great Company, 1667–1871. Being a History of the Honourable Company of Merchant Adventurers trading into Hudson's Bay. Beckles Willson (1900).

A Brief History of the Hudson's Bay Company. (Published by the Company 1957.)

The Remarkable History of the Hudson's Bay Company. G. Bryce (1900).

The North West Company. Marjorie Wilkins Campbell (1957).

The Royal African Company. K. G. Davies (1957).

The South Sea Bubble. L. Melville (1921).

The South Sea Bubble. Lord Erleigh (1933).

The South Sea Bubble. John Carswell (1960).

The South Sea House. Charles Lamb. (From the Essays of Elia.)

Mungo Park and the Quest of the Niger. Stephen Gwynn (1934).

Sir George Goldie and the Making of Nigeria. J. E. Flint (1960).

Sir George Goldie, Founder of Nigeria. Dorothy Wellesley and Stephen Gwynn (1934).

Lugard: the Years of Adventure. Margery Perham (1956).

Cecil Rhodes. B. Williams (1938).

Rhodes. Sarah G. Millin (1952).

The White Rajahs of Sarawak, 1841–1946. S. Runciman (1960).

Under Chartered Company Rule: North Borneo, 1881–1946. K. G. Tregonning (1958).

The Great Chartered Companies. David Hannay (1926).

Index